TALES OF THE EAST

VOLUME ONE

MYSTIC TALES FROM INDIA'S ENLIGHTENED CULTURE

MATTHEW F. BENNETT A.L.C.

MATURA NATH DAS ADHIKARI

Other books by the author:

Absolute Abundance

Dharma of Abundance

The Mystic Christ

Life After Life

For more information or to schedule a private consultation.

Please visit
www.abundantlives.org

ISBN-13: 978-1494905880

Editing / Proofreading: Sripad Rsabdev das,

Deva & Mayi Devi Dasi & Nabadwip das

Dedicated to the memory of my good friend Jaya Krsna das

ni sankoce bapana karena ya
ra bhaktimaya jivanera bija
ara ya ra raksa karena o lalana
karena se apurva bhaktilata bija
ya dera karunabalei matra
ei grantha halena
prakashitata deri shricarane
ami shrigrantha kari arpita

"This book is humbly dedicated to those
who fearlessly bestow the seed of spiritual life,
as well as those guardians who protect and
nurture the tender creeping vine of divine love.
By their mercy alone, this is manifest."

I make my prostrate obeisance unto my Guru Parampara:
His Divine Grace Srila Bhakti Raksaka Sridhar-Dev Goswami Maharaj
who is a transcendental treasure house of pure devotional conclusions.
To my siksa Gurudeva His Divine Grace Srila Bhakti Sundar Govinda-Dev
Goswami Maharaj who is the personification of pure devotion to His Gurudeva
and the greatest affectionate gaurdian for the aspiring devotees. To His Divine Grace
A. C. Bhaktivedanta Swami Maharaj who fearlessly introduced pure devotion
throughout the entire world.

blessed art thou upon the swan

the essence of divine sound
and everlasting beauty

inspiration of the speaker
poet & priest

the creator's beloved
and friend of the pure

your hands bear the vina
the book and the beads

while granting a boon

fulfilling our needs

an image auspicious

bright halo enshrined

grant us thy mercy

benevolence divine

CONTENTS

INTRODUCTION

Tales of the East is a compilation of folk tales and puranic histories, gleaned from ancient Vedic literatures which were first compiled by the great sage Vyasa some 5,000 years ago at the end of the *Dwapara-yuga* (the last great universal epoch).

Each wonderful and entertaining story reflects one facet of the mystic gem of spiritual truth, demonstrating various features of spiritual conduct, development, and ontology. Although these and countless other tales have been told and retold in India for many thousands of years, they possess such an inexhaustible spiritual vitality that people enjoy hearing them narrated again and again, engendering in listeners an ever-deepening understanding and appreciation for life, death and humanity's ultimate destiny.

In former ages the great Vedic wisdom was transmitted orally from guru to disciple in the tradition of sampradaya, or disciplic succession. At the onset of *Kali-yuga,* (the present age, said to continue for the next 400,000 years), the sage Vyasa, was prompted by his own guru, the celestial sage Narada (who appears in some of our tales), to commit the Vedas to writing for the benefit of those of us who would come later.

The spiritual concepts contained in the Vedic literatures are the realizations of enlightened sages. These enlightened sages, such as Vyasa, Narada, Asita, Devala and others rejected all religious activities which were materially motivated. By such pure intention they were enabled to clearly distinguish transcendent reality from worldly illusion, and the Vedas are their attempt to record a glimpse of that truth for the spiritual welfare of all peoples of the world.

1

The Vedic wisdom is believed to have spiritually existed eternally, and to have originally manifested in the material sphere as sound vibration which was then realized by perfected sages. The word veda, literally means "know this" (in an imperative sense) for it is considered axiomatic truth descending from the super subjective plane of absolute conscious reality.

Only with the aid of faith we can accept that the Vedas have a transcendent origin, their initial revelation being untainted by the constraints of materially conditioned thought. From the Vedas we receive knowledge of an Absolute Reality—a transcendent spiritual Godhead whose divine form is composed of eternity, knowledge and dynamic joy (sat, chit, ananda), and who's transcendent nature embraces the conception of both female and male transcendent attributes *(shakti & shaktiman)*. It is by the mercy of this Absolute Reality that all truth and knowledge are revealed, for within the Vedas it is stated that God is both the source and goal of the Vedas.

As is stated in the Vedic text Bhagavad-gita:

> vedais ca sarvair aham eva vedyam
> vedanta-krit vedavid-eva chaham

> *Bhagavad-gita 15.15*

"By all the Vedas I am to be known. Indeed, I am the compiler of Vedanta, and I am the knower of the Vedas."

This conception of Godhead, although transcending the limitations of mundane duality, paradoxically may contain inconceivable male and female divine attributes, revealing that God is not exclusively singular or monotheistic, but may also be inconceivably one and yet ultimately, a divine coupling of inconceivably personal spiritual principles. Often we conceive of God in a singular sense, yet if we are created in God's image, and that we consider we are ourselves surrounded by associates and family, then why should our conception of divinity deny the absolute divinity an ability to interact personally? This is not merely anthropomorphism, but another way of saying that whatever exists in the effect must also exist in the cause.

Therefore in the Vedic literatures we find the ultimate spiritual personality to be surrounded by innumerable members of a loving entourage and in this sense, the associates of God are His enlightened and liberated potencies, of both male and female characteristics. Furthermore, we find the potent dynamically engaged in divine affectionate play with these innumerable potencies *(lila)*.

The tales in this Edition are all in relation to this dynamic reality and will surely awaken a sense of wonder in the thoughtful reader, for God is the wonder of wonders and summum bonum of all truth, knowledge, beauty and affection.

Despite my personal lack of qualification, It is my hope that by the Grace of my Spiritual Masters this publication may be useful in conveying universal spiritual principles to everyone, regardless of their age, religious, cultural, racial or economic background. Such truths constitute real knowledge and can ultimately lead such thoughtful persons toward the supreme fulfillment of life: the heart's joyful unfolding in unmotivated, loving devotional activities whose aim it is to please an infinite, yet personal God— the Absolute Reality, Reality the Beautiful.

Matthew F. Bennett
Matura nath Das Adhikari

THE KING DESIRES A SON

In the state of Sura there lived a handsome and educated king named Chitra-ketu. Because he was righteous, the citizens were happy and the earth produced all the necessities of life in profusion. The king himself, however, was unhappy, for despite the fact that he had many beautiful wives he was unable to produce a son.

One day as the king sat upon his throne, the powerful sage Angira arrived at the palace. The king immediately arose from his throne and offered respect to the sage by bowing down in humility. He seated the sage upon comfortable pillows and offered him varieties of palatable foodstuffs.

This greatly pleased the sage, who spoke to the king as follows: "O King Chitra-ketu, I thank you for your hospitality and pray that you may achieve all good fortune. Your humility is certainly befitting one who knows the progressive values of life. Your kingdom and subjects appear happy and prosperous, yet I detect some discontent within you. Just as one may understand the inner condition of a fruit by examining its skin, similarly, one may know the condition of others' minds by analyzing their facial expressions. The face is often the indicator of the mind. By this I can understand that you are carrying sadness within you. Have you not achieved your desired goals in life? Are you not satisfied by your royal paraphernalia?"

The king replied: "O great sage, by dint of your austerities and transcendental knowledge, surely nothing remains unknown to you. Still, out of compassion for me you have inquired about my distress, so let me therefore disclose its cause to you. When a person is hungry and thirsty he cannot be satisfied by external paraphernalia such as clothing and jewelry. In a similar way, I remain unsatisfied by my royal position, wealth, education, and beautiful wives, because I have no son."

Smiling, the sage then said, "Fear not, O King." Then, desiring to relieve the anxiety of the king, the powerful sage prepared a medicinal mixture of special herbs and sweet rice and recited appropriate prayers. Thereafter, this rice was given to the king's foremost queen, Kritad-yuti. After the queen had eaten the rice, the sage made a cryptic prediction, saying, "O King, your queen shall now bear a son who will be the cause of both happiness and distress." So saying, the sage departed, and in the following months the queen developed in her pregnancy, just as the moon waxes full in the bright fortnight.

In due course of time a son was born to the king, and the entire kingdom resounded in jubilation. Great festivals and celebrations were held in honor of the child, and the king engaged learned priests in performing the royal birth ceremony. When a poor man achieves wealth after much difficulty, he certainly becomes very attached to that wealth. In the same way, the king's affection for his son grew daily. Naturally, the queen also became excessively attached to the boy, who was the center of attention throughout the palace.

The other queens of Chitra-ketu, however, became increasingly jealous of Kritad-yuti. For now, she and her son commanded all the affection and attention of the king. They could not bear the king's growing indifference towards them, and as a result their hearts burned with envy. As their envy increased, their intelligence and other good qualities diminished. In such a hard-hearted condition they secretly fed poison to the helpless child.

Some time later queen Kritad-yuti became concerned, thinking that the child had been sleeping for too long. She ordered the nursemaid to wake the child and bring him to her. But when the nursemaid approached the child, to her great horror she saw that the child's eyes were turned upward and he was not breathing. Thus, she understood that he was dead. The queen heard the nursemaid shriek and, running to the spot, she trembled in sorrow as she looked upon the dead body of her child. At that moment her heart was rent asunder by a lightning bolt of grief, and she cried out in anguish as she fell unconscious to the palace floor.

The king was also devastated by the news of his son's death. With his eyes shedding tears like torrents of rain he ran slipping and stumbling to the place where the dead child lay. As he stared in disbelief at the dead body of the child, the queen, her eyes brimming with tears, began to speak out in a tone of condemnation: "O Creator! You are certainly cruel, for within the lifetime of a father you have allowed the death of his son. Thus you have contradicted your own creative laws."

Then in an imploring and pitiful tone, she turned to the dead child and said, "O sweet child, please do not give up our company. Just look upon the face of your lamenting father, whose heart is wrenching in unbearable grief. You have slept for too long, my child; please arise from this slumber. Your playmates are calling you to join them. You must be very hungry now, so please come and take your lunch. Great sorrow has overtaken me, for I can no longer hear your sweet voice." As the king and queen lamented in this way, their grief increased like an unchecked conflagration of sorrow spreading to the hearts of all the servants and residents of the palace.

When the news of this tragedy reached the sage, he hastened to the palace in the company of his friend Narada. When they arrived, Angira and Narada found the king and queen merged in a deep ocean of sorrow, collapsed by the side of their son's dead body. With great compassion the two sages began to instruct the king in that type of spiritual knowledge which frees one from all misery. Angira said, "O King, please examine this situation carefully. What relationship do you have with this dead body which you are lamenting over? And what is its relationship with you? One may say that you are related as father and son, but did this relationship exist prior to its birth?

Does it really exist now? Shall it continue to exist in the future? O King, just as small grains of sand are repeatedly joined and separated by the force of the ocean's tides, the eternal living beings who have accepted temporary material bodies sometimes come together and at other times are separated by the force of time. Therefore, please do not lament over this temporary relationship of parenthood. All beings are unmanifest in their beginning, manifest in the interim, and again unmanifest at death.

These visible forms are merely the products of the external material energy of the Lord. When the eternal living soul mistakenly identifies with the temporary body, its intelligence becomes bewildered by the bodily concept of life; and although the soul is categorically different and superior to the body, through the agency of the mind, the soul unnecessarily suffers. The soul, however, is eternal and inexhaustible, and therefore one need not grieve for any creature. In the Vedic scriptures we find this clearly described:

avinashi tu tad viddhi
yena sarvam idam tatam
vinasham avyayasyasya
na kascit kartum arhati

"That soul which pervades the entire body is imperishable.
Being unchangeable and everlasting,
nothing can destroy him."

Bhagavad-gita 2.17

The king felt relieved to hear the instructions of the sage and, wiping the tears from his face, he said, "O sages, I thank you for your kind instructions. By your grace I have regained my composure. Great personalities like you are ever seeking to enlighten ignorant persons such as I. Those who are advanced in spiritual knowledge are never affected by loss or gain, for they understand that everything is created and controlled by the Supreme Lord." Angira then replied, "I could have given you this knowledge of transcendence when I first arrived at your palace, but I could understand that your mind was absorbed in the material desire for a son. Therefore I gave you a son who was the cause of both joy and sorrow, but actually all relationships and possessions are similar in that they are temporary. Due to their impermanent nature they have no more value than dreams."

Then, before the eyes of all the astonished onlookers, Narada, who was also a great sage and mystic, caused the soul of the dead child to reenter its lifeless body by the power of his mystic potency. This is called *mritasan jivani*, the power to restore life. Narada then spoke to the child in this way: " O living soul, may all good fortune be yours. Please look upon your grieving friends and relatives, who are saddened by your premature passing from this world. Because of your untimely death, the unlived balance of your life remains. Therefore I direct you to reenter your body, and request that you resume the remainder of your life in the company of your loving family members and friends. Your mother and father await you, so please get up."

To the wonder of all, the child slowly sat up and began to speak in words that were saturated with wisdom. He said, "By the inevitable results of my own activities and the evolution of my consciousness, I, the eternal soul, transmigrate through various species of life. Sometimes I enjoy the heavenly position of a demigod, and at other times I suffer the confinement of animal existence. Sometimes I take birth among the plants and trees, and at other times I am born into a human form. No one is actually my father and mother, for I am a spiritual soul who exists independent of these material forms. So you must kindly tell me in which birth these two persons were my father and mother. Otherwise, how is it possible for me to really accept them as such?

"This material world behaves like a swiftly moving river that carries away the living beings who are immersed in its waves. All people assume the roles of friends, relatives, and enemies throughout the course of time. And according to the nature of these relationships they behave in either a friendly or hostile manner towards one another.

But despite these various interactions, no one is permanently related. Just as goods are transferred from place to place in the course of their purchase and sale, the soul is similarly transferred through various bodily forms by dint of the weight or merit of its actions. This is achieved by being repeatedly injected into various bodies by one father after another. Yet the living being is eternal and indestructible, without beginning or end. In reality, the soul never takes birth or dies, although externally it may appear that way to those who are materially conditioned.

Although the soul is the basis for different types of bodies, it never belongs to the category of material energy of which the body is constructed. Although subordinate to God, the soul is of a similar spiritual nature, because it is an expansion of the marginal potency of God, just as a particle of sunshine is the potency of the sun planet. The soul is not materially quantifiable, and therefore, due to its minute size, it is prone to illusion and bewilderment by the external material energy of God. Thus by the force of various material desires the soul creates different types of bodies for itself which bring about its experience of the dualities of happiness and distress." After speaking in this way, the soul once again departed from the body of the child.

All present there were dumbfounded by the speech of the child. Being cleansed of their lamentation by the potency of spiritual knowledge, they looked at one another in astonishment. The spell of illusory affection had been utterly broken, and they now began to prepare the child's body for cremation. The envious queens who had poisoned the child felt so ashamed that they gave up all ambition to bear children. Remembering the instructions of the sages, they went to the bank of the Yamuna River where, accompanied by priests, they atoned for their sin by engaging in penance.

By the instructions of the sages, the king became spiritually enlightened and, as an elephant emerges from a muddy lake, he emerged from the illusory affections of family life. The sages then initiated the king into the practice of spiritual life by imparting to him the mantra, *namas tubhya bhagavate, vasudevaya sat cit ananda dhimahi:* "O my Lord, O all-pervading God, I bow down to You and meditate upon Your spiritual form of eternity, knowledge, and bliss."

After practicing this mantra for some time, the king became perfected in spiritual realization and eventually attained a vision of the Lord. The Supreme Spiritual Personality, Who is super-subjective and beyond all mundane conception, gracefully revealed His beautiful divine form of unparalleled spiritual ecstasy to the king, who in turn offered choice prayers for the Lord's satisfaction. By the blessings of the Lord, Chitra-ketu was completely freed from the ignorance that gives rise to material suffering.

All material dualities have their origin in sensory perception. But by the grace of the Lord one attains bhakti-prema, or devotional love of God, which includes atma-jnana. Atma-jnana means self-knowledge—by which one can understand the eternal position of one's own individual spiritual self and simultaneously re-awaken the eternal relationship of loving reciprocation with

God, who is all-good, and all merciful. Being thus situated, one gradually transcends material dualities.

matra-sparsas tu kaunteya
stitoshna-sukha-dukha-da
agamapayino nityas
tams titiksasva bharata

"O son of Kunti, by the action of sense perception one experiences the temporary dualities of happiness and distress, heat and cold, pleasure and pain. These come and go like the seasons. Therefore, knowing them to be temporary, just try to endure them with an equipoised mind."

Bhagavad-gita 2.14

THE MYSTIC KING

After being directly blessed by the Supreme Lord, the former king Chitra-ketu quit his gross physical body and became a very powerful mystic yogi. Because he had achieved a subtle ethereal existence, his form and strength were practically free from deterioration and, as a result, he enjoyed heavenly pleasure for an incalculable amount of time. In the valleys of the heavenly Mount Sumeru he would chant the glories of the Lord in the company of beautiful heavenly maidens.

One time the yogi was travelling through the sky, seated upon a mystically airborne conveyance that had been given to him by Lord Vishnu. As he was flying here and there singing the praises of God, he came upon an assembly of saints and perfected beings engaged in discussing spiritual topics. In the center of this assembly was Lord Shiva, the great Maha-deva and seated on his lap was his wife, Parvati.

When the yogi saw Lord Shiva embracing Parvati, he laughed very loudly and spoke in such a way that was overheard by the assembly. The yogi said: "Lord Shiva is the best of all devotees of the Lord and the leader of those who know the religious conclusions of the scriptures; therefore it is certainly unusual to see him shamelessly embracing his wife within the view of so many saintly persons." Lord Shiva was not affected by this apparently offensive statement of the yogi.

Because Lord Shiva is extremely powerful and endowed with unlimited knowledge, he could understand the yogi's purpose in making such a statement; therefore he simply smiled and remained silent. The sages and perfected beings present in the assembly could also understand the reason for the yogi's statement and, therefore, they too remained silent. Because

Lord Shiva is the greatest devotee of the Supreme Lord and the most powerful of all the demigods, he is able to act in any way he desires.

Although he was apparently disregarding proper etiquette, his exalted position is never diminished by such actions. The yogi, however, was afraid that if common persons saw Lord Shiva's behavior, they would misunderstand the situation and mistakenly follow that example. This idea is represented in the scriptures as well:

yad yad acarati shresthas
tat tad evetaro janah
sa yat pramanam kurute
lokas tad anuvartate

"Whatever actions are performed by great men, those same actions will be adopted by common men. And whatever standards are accepted by the great, that also the whole world shall pursue."

Bhagavad-gita 3.21

Although there may have been good intentions behind the yogi's statement, its delivery was improper, for one should never attempt to publicly instruct or correct the behavior of a superior personality, especially one so exalted as Lord Shiva. By making this statement the yogi seemingly minimized Shiva's position, and this angered Parvati, who then said, "Alas, by whose authority does this impudent fool come to judge the actions of Lord Shiva, who is the personification of religious qualities? Indeed, all the demigods and sages bow their heads to the holy feet of Lord Shiva; yet this person dares to criticize my lord? Let him be punished immediately!"

Then, turning to the yogi, Parvati continued, "O haughty child,

I curse you to fall from your heavenly situation and take birth in a lowly and sinful family of wrong-doers. By this you shall be purified of your offense and thus learn a valuable lesson regarding proper conduct towards saintly persons."Realizing his blunder, the yogi immediately descended from his conveyance. With gestures of submission he spoke to Mother Parvati and said, "O Mother, with all due respect, I wholly accept your curse upon me. Indeed, happily I shall bear this burden, for both pleasure and pain are awarded by the demigods as a result of one's own past actions.

Bewildered by ignorance, living beings wander throughout this world encountering the joys and sorrows that are merely the products of their own desires and actions. Therefore no one is to be blamed for this incident. My happiness and distress are destined by my previous actions, and therefore I do not seek to escape this curse. However, I humbly request you to excuse my offense towards Lord Shiva and your good self." After speaking in this way the yogi took leave of that assembly and, as Lord Shiva and Parvati looked on, he departed in the sky.

Lord Shiva and Parvati were astonished at the behavior of the yogi and, realizing that he was unafraid despite being cursed, they smiled with great satisfaction. Then Lord Shiva began to speak of the glories of the devotees of the Supreme Lord, saying, "My dear wife, today we have witnessed the greatness of the saints. Because they are servants of the Supreme Personality of Godhead, they are naturally enriched with perfect knowledge and detachment from this material world. Therefore they are never affected by happiness and distress." Then the great Lord Shiva uttered this mantra:

narayana-para sarve
na kutashcana bibhyati
svargapavarga-narakeshev
api tulyartha-darshina

"Those who are engaged in the service of the Supreme Lord are never fearful of any adverse condition of life. These great personalities are solely interested in the Lord's service and thus consider heaven, hell, and liberation to be equally insignificant."

Srimad Bhagavatam 6.17.28

THE GOOD TAILOR

Once, in India, near the town of Bendel, there lived a gentle tailor. By stitching clothes this gentleman would earn enough money to maintain himself, and the other half of his earnings he would use in the service of God.

One regular customer of the tailor was in the habit of paying the tailor with counterfeit coins. Although the tailor knew the coins to be false, he nonetheless quietly accepted them. One day the tailor had to go out to pick up some cloth for the preparation of garments. At that time he left his assistant in charge of the shop.

A short time later the customer arrived to pick up some garments and, as usual, he offered false coins for the cloth. The assistant became angry and told the man to pay with real money. When the tailor returned some time later, the assistant told him: "A man came this morning and tried to deceive me with false coins."

The tailor replied, "Oh yes, I know him. You should have taken the coins." The assistant was bewildered at such a reply, until the tailor explained. "I regularly accept the false coins from that man and throw them in the river; if I do not accept them, then others may be cheated." The assistant had studied the scriptures in the company of this saintly tailor and recalled one verse from his lessons:

> titiksava karu nika su
> surida sarva-dehinam
> ajata-shatrava santa
> sadhava sadhu-bhusa na

"The symptoms of a sadhu (saint) are that he is tolerant, merciful, and friendly to all living entities. He has no enemies, he is peaceful, he abides by the scriptures, and all his characteristics are sublime."

Srimad-Bhagavatam 3.25.2

CLOSE TO THE CENTER

In a small village by the banks of the holy Yamuna River, a man was making flour by using a grinding stone. As he crushed the wheat grains in the stone mortar, he reflected within himself how he too was being crushed by the miseries of worldly life. He felt great sadness within his heart and began to shed tears.

Just at that moment the great sage Narada happened to be passing by on his way to the river. Seeing the man crying, the saint asked of him, "Brother, why do you cry?" The man replied that like the grains of wheat in his mortar, he also felt that he was being crushed by the weight of his worldly life. Narada then requested him to lift the upper grinding stone and pointed out how the grains near the center peg remained whole, while those that moved away from the center were powdered. Narada then said, "By serving the interest of Divinity, Who is the center of existence, you will remain close to Him, and by remaining close to Him, you shall not suffer the weight of adversities of this worldly life, just as these grains near the center peg are uncrushed." Narada then recited this verse from the scriptures:

mac-citta sarva-durgani
mat-prasadat tarisyasi
atha cet tvam ahankaran
na sroshyasi vinankyasi

"When your heart is ever devoted to Me, you shall overcome all obstacles of conditioned life by My grace. If, however, out of pride you disregard My words, then surely you shall be misguided and suffer greatly."

Bhagavad-gita 18.58

THE BOY WHO WON A KINGDOM

Yamun-acharya was the foremost exponent of Shri Vaishnavism (devotional piety to the personal aspect of Godhead) before Ramanuja. Born about 953 A.D. in Madurai, the capital of the kingdom of Pandura, Yamun-acharya was raised by his mother and grandmother, as his father had passed away, and his grandfather Natha-muni had taken sannyasa, or the renounced order of life. As a child he had a sweet and gentle nature and excelled in his studies raising himself far above his admiring contemporaries. He was a scholarly genius who amazed everyone and due to his proficiency and diligence he became the favorite of his teacher Bhasya-charya.

By the power of his intelligence Yamun-acharya gained a kingdom by charming the royal court of the king of Kola and defeating the royal pundit (scholar) who was famous as 'Vidvaj-jana-kola-hala,' meaning "thrower of scholars into an uproar." Because the royal pundit was very dear to the king, he was patronized lavishly, and this proud royal pandit used to exact a yearly tax from the subordinant scholars in the land. Scholars who could not pay this tax had to face the proud royal pundit in open debate and face public humiliation as punishment. Fearing the loss of thier academic reputations as scholars, all of them would regularly pay this tax in fear of losing thier scholarly prestiege. Yamuna acharya's guru hapened to be away one day when an agent of the royal pundit arrived at the ashram and solicited payment of the tax.

Yamun-acharya, who was only twelve at the time, was angered by the demand for tax considering it an insult to the ashram, his lineage and the dignity of his guru. Because of this, Yamuna acharya refused to pay the tax to the collector and sent him back with a challenge that an insignificant follower of Bhasya-charya would face the proud world-conquering royal pundit in an open debate before the royal assembly.

The royal pundit was humorously suprised and laughed alot at the thwelve year old boy's challenge and had the young scholar summoned to the royal court. O the day of the debate the king sent a regal palanquin to bring the young challenger and when the queen first set eyes upon the beautiful boy she was instantly captivated by his sweetness and youthful courage. Secretly in her heart she took the side of the charming boy and prayed that he might defeat the arrogant pandit who had been favored so long by the king. Soon after, the queen could not conatin her enthusiasm and a bet was made between the king and queen that if the boy lost the debate to the pandit, the queen would have to indulge the king's every whim, and if the boy were to win, the king would bestow half of his kingdom upon the boy.

The royal pundit examined the boy, and inquired of him many obscure questions about Sanskrit grammar which the boy answered with great alacrity and precision. When it was the boy's turn to examine the royal pandit He said, "Allow me to state three precepts for your consideration. Refute them if you can! "My first statement is: your mother is not barren." Hearing this audacious remark the royal pundit was momentarily stunned. For he realized if he were to refute this statement he would be denying his own birth. Silently trembling with smoldering rage, he could not speak or move in his embarrassment, shocked by the cleverness of this young boy.

Yamun-acharya then stated, "My second proposal is this: the king is pious. Please refute this statement if you dare." Hearing this second clever statement the pandit was shocked beyond belief. He realized that it would be impossible to prove his own patron king was impious. How could he possibly present such an argument without insulting the king. Then for the third proposal the boy scholar said, "Here is my third statement: the queen is chaste. If you can refute this statement I will gladly admit defeat."

Unable to refute these propositions, the pundit became frustrated and angry, and in desperation he said, "You are proposing things which are irrefutable. By asking me to challenge the piety of the king and the chastity of the queen you are committing treason and blasphemy! How dare you ask this of me! This is an outrage. If you think these propositions can be refuted, then refute them yourself and be condemned as an offender to the throne. Otherwise admit your insolence and hang your head in shame."

The pundit's followers filled the arena with applause, and the king felt confident that his champion had successfully turned back the challenge of this impudent boy. But the boy was not finished. "As you wish," he said. "I shall refute these propositions myself. First I asked you to refute the proposal that your mother is not barren. Since you have failed to do so, I must cite the Manu Smrti on this matter. According to the laws of Manu,

Eka-putro hy aputrena lokavadat:

"If a woman has no more than one child,
she may be considered barren."

Manu-Samhita 9.61, Medhatithi Bhasya

Since your mother had only one son, the proposal that she is not barren is refuted. "Now the second proposal: the king is pious. I asked you to refute this, but you were unable to do so. The laws of Manu also state that since a king is responsible for the protection of his subjects, he assumes one-sixth of the results of their pious and impious deeds.

Sarvato dharmashaya bhago rajo bhavati rakshatah, adharmadapi shaya bhago bhavatyasya hyarakshatah:

Manu-Samhita 8.304, Medhatithi Bhasya.

Since this is Kali-yuga, the people in general are naturally impious, and so the king must assume a heavy burden of impiety. This refutes the second thesis that the king is pious.

"As for my refutation of the third proposal that the queen is chaste...." With this the crowd became quiet, and the queen herself blushed. The boy's supporters wondered how he could refute this proposition and conquer the pundit without embarrassing the queen. Yamun-acharya continued, "The laws of Manu state that a great king is the representative of the demigods. The gods—Agni the fire-god, Vayu the wind-god, Surya the sun-god, Chandra the moon-god, Yamaraja the lord of death, Varuna the lord of water, Kuvera the lord of wealth, and Indra—are all present in the body of the king. The queen, therefore, is wedded to more than just one man. When a woman is married to more than one man, how then can she be chaste? Thus the third proposition is refuted."

The crowd was astonished. The boy scholar had certainly defeated the royal pundit. The queen was jubilant and embraced the boy, saying, "Alaban-daru," meaning "one who conquers." The royal pundit was disgraced. The king, who had been defeated in his wager with the queen, arose and said, "My boy Alaban-daru, child-scholar, you have defeated my royal pundit—the terror of all scholars, Vidvaj-jana-kola-hala himself. His pitiful life is now yours to do with as you see fit. I commend him into your hands. As for yourself, I promised the queen to give you half my kingdom upon your victory here. Now that you have won, I humbly request you to accept half my kingdom as your reward." The king then awarded the boy a beautiful palace filled with riches and maintained by hundreds of servants.

Yamun-acharya, who had won the title of 'conqueror,' now became famous as Alaban-daru the boy-king. As the years passed he became involved more and more in the affairs of state, practically forgetting the legacy of his grandfather Natha-muni. Surrounded by kingly opulence and royal power, he gradually became entrenched in the position of a king. Absorbed in politics, he had little time for spiritual affairs.

Around this time, Natha-muni passed away; but before he left this world, he called his most confidential disciple Nambi to his side and entrusted him with a sacred task— to go and inspire Yamun-acharya to renounce his kingdom and champion the cause of Shri Vaishnavism. Yamun-acharya was uniquely qualified to propagate this concept of devotion to a personal Godhead; no one else could take the place of Natha-muni.

Years passed. Finally the time came to spur Yamun-acharya into action. Nambi, remembering the order of his guru, set out to confront Yamun-acharya and convince him of the need to renounce material life and teach the philosophy of Sri Vaisnavism. When he arrived at the palace gates, however, he was turned away. It was not easy for a humble mendicant to get an interview with the great king Alaban-daru. Therefore Nambi devised an alternate plan. Through inquiry, he came to know who the royal cook was. One day, while the cook was returning from the marketplace with fresh produce, Nambi stopped him and gave him some fresh vegetable greens called tuduvali, which are said to promote mental purity and increase one's tendency towards contemplation and spiritual life. He asked the cook to please prepare these greens regularly for the welfare of the king, and the pious cook, understanding the rarity and purity of these greens, said he would be pleased to do so. From that day on the cook began regularly preparing the greens for the king's lunch. The king very much enjoyed the greens, and Nambi would regularly supply them to the cook.

One day, Nambi held back. The king missed his greens and asked the cook why they had not been prepared. When the cook explained about the mysterious mendicant who supplied these greens, the king's interest was piqued. "The next time this man comes," the king ordered his royal cook, "bring him before me." The next day when Nambi returned with the greens, the cook brought him before the king and introduced him. "What do you want of me?" the king asked. "Why do you supply these greens everyday for no payment?" Nambi requested a private audience. The king ordered all his attendants to leave them alone, and when everyone had gone he offered Nambi a seat. "Please speak," he said. Nambi then told the king of his grandfather's passing. He told him of Natha-muni's anxiety that the disciplic family of Shri Vaishnavism needed a champion, a great scholar who could defeat opposing schools of philosophy and establish the religious principles of their tradition.

Only Yamun-acharya was qualified to do this, but he had now become a great king, a ruler of men attached to royal luxury and power. Gradually Nambi awoke in the king's heart a desire to renounce the throne and lead the disciplic family. After deeply considering the message of Bhagavad-gita in Nambi's company, Yamun-acharya visited the temple of Shri Rangam, where he accepted mantra initiation from Nambi and committed himself to giving up the opulence of royalty and taking up the mission of his grandfather.

After surrendering himself fully to a life of spiritual discipline, meditation and devotion, Yamuna-charya went on to become a great teacher. He quickly became the intellectual and spiritual leader of the Shri Vaishnavas, and was highly regarded for his realization, his scholarship, and his synthesis of Natha-muni's system of philosophy with the system of worship ordained by the Vedas. Yamuna-charya's unquestioned status as a brahmin helped him to establish his version of Vedanta above the protests of the impersonalist followers of Shankar-acharya.

Thus he increased the prestige of devotional service to God by demonstrating both its scriptural basis and spiritual superiority to the mundane caste system. Among his writings are the famous devotional prayers to Lord Vishnu known as the Stotra-ratna, the "Jewel of Prayers," in which he says:

bhavantam evanucaran nirantarah
prashanta-nih shesha-manorathantarah
kadaham aikantika-nitya-kinkarah
praharshayishyami sa-natha-jivitam

"By serving You constantly, one is freed from all material desires and is completely pacified. When shall we be engaged as Your eternal servant and always feel joyful to have such a perfect master?"

Stotra-ratna, verse 45

MONKEY BUSINESS

In the foothills of the Himalayas near the holy city of Rishikesh there lived a brahmin boy whose name was Gopal das. His parents had passed away and, since that time, he lived in a modest hut on the banks of the Ganges River, ever chanting the holy names of God. He received food from the ashram of his guru, who was very pleased by the boy's humility and service attitude. Every day Gopal would perform service to his guru by collecting firewood and flowers from the forest and delivering them to the guru's ashram.

One day after finishing his service, Gopal sat down beneath a tree to take his noon meal of mango fruits. Soon a pack of monkeys appeared and began to eye Gopal's lunch. One monkey ran very quickly and, before Gopal could prevent him, the monkey snatched Gopal's last mango. The other monkeys became envious and hotly pursued the monkey with the mango until finally, in exhausted desperation the monkey threw it to the ground.

Then another monkey would quickly snatch up the mango and the others would doggedly harass him. In this way none of the monkeys actually enjoyed the mango, because the possessor and the pursuers were both constantly agitated by the desire to possess the fruit. As Gopal watched in amazement, the monkeys repeated this scenario over and over again.

After finishing his meal, Gopal returned to the ashram and related the story of the monkeys to his guru. The guru simply smiled and said, "Just like the monkeys, when we neglect the service of the Lord and simply seek to satisfy our own personal desires, so many conflicts arise between human beings, and neither party actually benefits from such selfish actions." Then he spoke one appropriate verse from the Gita just for Gopal's instruction:

apuryam am acala-pratistham
samudram apa pravicanti yadvat
tadvat kama yaµ pravicanti sarve
sa cantim apnoti na kama-kami

"A person who is not disturbed by the incessant flow of desires—that enter like rivers into the ocean, which is ever being filled but is always still—can alone achieve peace, and not the man who strives to satisfy such desires."

Bhagavad-gita 2.70

BALA THE CLEVER CHILD

Long ago there lived a man named Rudra whose wife had died in childbirth. In the course of time Rudra again married, and from then on his son was raised by the second wife. Being of an envious nature and desiring to promote the status of her own son, she fed the orphaned child stale foodstuffs that were hard and lacking in nutritional quality. As a result the young boy became emaciated with a swollen stomach and projecting bones.

Upon noticing the unattractive features of the boy, Rudra questioned him about his condition, yet the boy made no complaint. From that time on he called the boy Bala-vinas-taka (one whose strength is lost when he is a boy). To the amazement of all, he showed great intelligence although he was but a boy of five years. One day he thought it time to teach his stepmother a lesson.

At the end of the day as his father Rudra relaxed in a chair, Bala climbed onto his lap as children often do. With an ingenious air the boy said to his father, "Father, I have two fathers." Rudra was surprised by this remark, and at first thought it to be nothing more than childish baby-talk. He tried to dismiss the child's remark from his mind but, being unable to do so, found himself growing jealous and doubtful of his wife's character.

He thought she must be seeing a secret lover, so, from then on, he never spoke to her. The stepmother was aware of the little boy's keen intelligence and therefore suspected Bala to be the cause of this change in her husband's behavior. One day she called the boy to her side and gently asked if he knew the reason for his father's change of behavior towards her. Bala told her

29

that if she would agree to feed and care for him properly in the future, then he would bring about a favorable change in his father's demeanor. To this proposal she gladly agreed.

Later that day when Rudra returned from his evening ablution in the Ganges River, the boy held a mirror before his father. When the reflection of his father appeared in the mirror, he said, "Father, I have two fathers." Immediately the doubts of his father were removed, and both father and son smiled in great satisfaction.

niti bale tara ababgar patra keu nay
krodh o lobher bashabarti jar hriday

"As a rule, none should be treated with indifference
actuated by greed or anger."

Valmiki Ramayana

VISIT TO A HOLY PLACE

Tukaram was a South Indian saint of renown who lived about five hundred years ago, and had been initiated into the devotional practice of chanting of the holy names of God by Chaitanya Mahaprabhu, the Golden Avatar, who travelled throughout India chanting the holy names of Lord Krishna. Because of his devotional sincerity, Tukaram's fame spread far and wide.

Once, some local villagers were preparing to go on pilgrimage to various holy sites and requested the saint to accompany them. The saint was unable to join them at that time and, after thanking them for their kind invitation, made a strange request of them. He said, "My friends, I am unable to go just now, but please take this bitter melon with you on your pilgrimage, carry it with you throughout your journey, and whether you are walking, resting, or worshiping in the temples, or even while you are taking bath in the holy rivers—always keep it with you."

Some of the pilgrims looked at one another with a puzzled look, thinking the request to be a bit eccentric, but knowing him to be a saint they respected his wish.

The pilgrims obeyed the request of the saint and faithfully carried the bitter gourd wherever they went. Taking turns, they carried it to every temple, and also submerged it in every holy river. After several months had passed, the pilgrims returned to the village of the saint and gave him back the bitter melon. With a smile he invited all the pilgrims to a feast to celebrate the completion of their pilgrimage.

The saint then made a special preparation from the bitter melon that had been carried by the pilgrims; as they all sat in a circle, he served it out to them. But as soon as they tasted the bitter melon preparation, they began to complain about its strong bitter taste. In wonder they asked the saint, "Why have you served us this terribly bitter and unripe melon?"

As if surprised, the saint replied, "O friends, this melon has been to all the temples and holy places, and has been dipped in all the sacred rivers; how can any bitterness remain within it?" The pilgrims then realized the purpose behind the saint's actions.

The saint then said, "It is not enough to simply carry one's body to various holy places yet all the while remaining unchanged within. Nor does the experience of the eyes constitute the realization of truth. When visiting a holy place, one must seek out the saints who reside there and take beneficial instructions from those holy persons. This is the true meaning of pilgrimage."

tad viddhi pranipatena
pariprashnena sevaya
upadekshyanti te jnanam
jnaninas tattva-darshinah

"You will attain knowledge of the truth by satisfying the saint who is well-situated in that knowledge. Offer your respects to him, and inquire from him submissively. By rendering service unto him, he shall be pleased to impart unto you all the truths which he has realized."

Bhagavad-gita 4.34

THE PEACEFUL BRAHMIN

There once was an educated brahmin who lived humbly in the forest with his wife and child. Their home was a simple thatched hut, but was beautified by the natural opulence that surrounded it. The brahmin was a very devoted and pious man who maintained his family by growing fruits and vegetables. He knew that the environment was ever controlled by the will of the Supreme Lord, for he was well educated in the Upanishads which state: ishavashyam idam sarvam. "Everything within the universe is owned and controlled by the Lord." Therefore, he always remained peaceful, never thinking himself the proprietor of anything, but ever dependent on the mercy of the Lord.

One day his young child fell ill with a burning fever. The brahmin and his wife attended the sick child for two days straight until the fever broke and the boy appeared to be recovering. By the third day the brahmin was exhausted. Thinking the child to be recovered, he went to take his rest. Quickly he fell into a deep sleep and rested the whole night until the early hours of the morning, when he was awakened by the weeping of his wife. It seems that despite their efforts the little boy had unexpectedly passed away in the night, and the mother was beside herself with grief.

The brahmin, however, remained undisturbed and went about his morning ablutions. Next, he calmly worshiped the Lord as was his daily habit. By noon he had prepared the funeral pyre and readied himself to conduct the last rites for the dead child. All throughout the morning his wife had bitterly wept for the lost child and by noon was furious at the apparent indifference shown by the brahmin. Finally, in anger she shouted at her husband, "How can you remain so calm! Don't you realize your only child has passed away? Are you so stone-hearted and cruel that you show no emotion?"

To which the brahmin replied, "Dear lady, of course I feel sadness at the loss of my child! But last night I had the most astonishing dream; please hear of it now."

"I dreamt that I was a king who was married to a beautiful queen, who along with seven affectionate children smothered me with their love. They played games with me, climbed atop my shoulders, hung about my neck, and sat upon my lap. I told stories to these children and affectionately embraced them all, but suddenly I awoke and found that the dream had vanished. Now today, I find that one son of mine has died, yet I wonder whether I should lament his loss, or the loss of the seven children in my dream! The outward material forms, be they subtle or gross, are all perishable and subject to transformation; but the soul is eternal and remains ever unaffected by these transformations. The Bhagavad-gita reminds us of these truths:

avyakto yam acintyo yam
avikaryo yam ucyate
tasmad evam viditvainam
nanushocitum arhasi

"It is said that the soul is invisible, inconceivable, immutable, and unchangeable. Knowing this, you should not grieve for the body."

Bhagavad-gita 2.25

SHIFTING THE BURDEN

In the north of India near an ancient temple, there lived a simple man named Chandra who sold banana leaves for a living. He would cleverly fashion them into plates by weaving twigs to hold them together. This he had done for many years, despite the fact that he was afflicted by painful bouts of arthritis. His friend Naresh was a clay cup maker, and sometimes the two would sell their wares together, hoping to fetch a higher price. Naresh was troubled by a bad leg and often told his friend, "If only I could exchange my bad leg for your arthritis I would be so much happier to be able to walk straight and tall." But Chandra would chastise him, saying, "Our woes are the results of our own activities, for every man suffers or enjoys the results of his own karma. Let me tell you of a dream I once had; please hear me attentively." As Naresh listened closely, Chandra began his tale.

Chandra said, "Once I dreamt that all the people of the world were gathered together in one place. They all cried out in sorrow, each one dissatisfied with his own condition and thinking that if they could exchange it with their neighbor, their life would be much improved. The Supreme Lord, who could hear their lamentations, appeared before them in a spiritual form of unequalled beauty, shining with the radiance of a thousand suns. The Lord said to them, 'O My children, I grant you the power that each one of you may cast off your particular affliction which is the source of your misery.'

"Quickly the assembled people began to throw off their burdens of sorrow and misery until the pile resembled a huge mountain. Then the Lord said to them, 'Now you may each pick up from this pile any burden or sorrow which you would like to exchange for your own.' A furious scramble ensued in which one person traded his particular trouble for that of his neighbor until the pile disappeared, and each person seemed satisfied and for the moment relieved. Then the Lord disappeared and each person returned to his home thinking his own condition much improved. "But the very next day, even louder cries were heard! All the people of the world gathered together once again and cried out, 'O Lord, please help us! Let us have our own sorrows back, for we cannot endure the pain which we have received in exchange!' The Lord again appeared and granted their wish, and with satisfaction they all accepted their previous afflictions.

They said to the Lord: 'We can now see our mistake, for we desired to be relieved of our sorrows in a way that resembles the shifting of a burden from one shoulder to another. Our sorrows are the results of our own selfish activities, and to follow the path of another is dangerous. Though our present positions may be painful, it is better to endure our own karma rather than accept another's lot. Let us therefore be engaged in Your service and purified of our selfish desires, and in that way be naturally relieved of the painful afflictions that result from them.' This pleased the Lord, who then smiled so beautifully that it enchanted all the worlds. Just then I awoke and taking the book by my bedside, to my astonishment I had randomly opened it to this verse:

karma-jam buddhi-yukta hi
phalam tyaktva manishina
janma-bandha-vinirmukta
padam gacchanty anamayam

'Those who are wise engage in devotional actions by taking shelter of the Lord. By such selfless activities they are released from the bondage of birth and death and attain to that divine peace which lies beyond all material miseries.'"

Bhagavad-gita 2.5

THE DESCENT OF GANGA

During the time of Lord Rama, this story of Ganga's descent was told to Lord Rama and His brother Lakshman by the sage Vishva-mitra as they all sat by the edge of the holy river Ganga. Vishva-mitra recounted the story as follows: Sagara of Ayodhya, who was a king of the solar dynasty, had for a long time been desirous of begetting a son to carry on his lineage. For this purpose he and his two wives, Keshini and Sumati, travelled to the Himalayas to perform austerities, where they encountered the sage Brighu. The sage was pleased with the humility of the king and blessed him, saying, "You shall attain unending fame and have a great number of sons.

One of your wives will bear only one child, who shall carry on your line, and the other shall give birth to sixty thousand powerful sons." The queens of Sagara both bowed before the sage and humbly inquired which would bear the one son, and which would bear the sixty thousand. The sage then asked them to make known their desires. Keshini said, "I will be satisfied with only one son, if he shall indeed carry on the line of kings." Sumati then said, "Please let me bear the sixty thousand sons, that I may populate the world with handsome and courageous princes." The sage then smiled and said, "Let it be so."

The king was very satisfied by all of this and happily returned with his wives to his capital of Ayodhya. According to the prediction of the sage, a son named Asam-anjas was born to Keshini, and Sumati gave birth to a huge mass of flesh that miraculously divided itself into sixty thousand babies. As the years slowly passed, the sixty thousand sons of Sumati grew up to be strong, handsome, and good-natured princes, whereas Asam-anjas developed a deranged personality and was considered a vicious madman. For entertainment he would drown little children in the river and merrily laugh as they helplessly struggled and died. In due course he was banished from the country, but not before he had produced a son. To the relief of all, this boy was nothing like his father. His name was Am-shuman, and he was as brave and virtuous as a young prince could be.

Once, as was the custom of ancient Vedic kings, Sagara desired to establish himself as sovereign of the world. This entailed sending out a challenge horse to all the kings of the surrounding countries. If these kings wished to challenge the superiority of Sagara, they would have to capture the horse and subsequently engage in battle with King Sagara.

As the king was preparing, he placed the challenge horse in the care of prince Am-shuman. But Indra, the foremost of demigods in heaven, desired to check the pride of the king, and so in the disguise of a hunter he stole the horse as it grazed in a pasture near the seashore. The king was very upset to hear the news of the missing horse and in great anxiety dispatched the sixty thousand sons of Sumati in search of it, commanding the princes: "Spare nothing to recover that horse. Wherever it may be, recover it at all costs!"

With great earnestness the princes ransacked the entire world without regard for anyone's personal property and, as a result, disturbed many people. They even dug huge holes in the earth as if searching for buried treasure. But despite their exhaustive search they failed to locate the horse anywhere. In frustration the king sent them to search the nether world of Patala.

Upon reaching that distant place they finally located the horse tied to a pole near the residence of the sage Kapila, the incarnation of Lord Vishnu who was seated there in silent meditation. In their haste the princes thought Kapila to be the thief and considered that He was simply pretending to be a yogi in meditation. They drew their swords and rushed toward Kapila shouting, "Capture the thief!" Kapila had been meditating for a long time and, as a result, was rich in tapo-bala, the subtle power achieved from the performance of austerities. Hearing the shouting of the boisterous princes, He simply opened His eyes and immediately the sixty thousand princes were reduced to ashes! This pleased Indra, for he had cleverly placed the horse in Kapila's ashram with this outcome in mind.

By now a long time had passed, and the king became impatient. Thinking some tragedy had befallen the sons of Sumati he sent his grandson Am-shuman in search of his sixty thousand uncles. Am-shuman followed the path of the princes, which finally led him to the residence of Kapila. To his delight he found the horse contentedly grazing there but was perplexed by the heaps of ashes everywhere. Garuda, who was the brother of Sumati, the kings's second wife, happened to be visiting Kapila at that time. He informed Am-shuman that the ashes were all that remained of his uncles. Garuda said, "Dear boy, these ashes are the remains of the sixty thousand princes.

They were incinerated as a result of their offenses to Kapila. Please return this horse to your father now so that he may complete his challenge. As far as your uncles are concerned, their ashes must be merged with the holy waters of the Ganga so that they may be purified of their offenses; then their souls may ascend to heaven. For that purpose Ganga must be brought down from Deva-loka, the abode of the demigods. By the blessings of Kapila all these things will come to pass." Am-shuman then respectfully approached Kapila and offered him gentle prayers. Kapila was pleased by his submissive behavior and, blessing him with encouraging words, bade him to take the challenge horse.

Am-shuman was exhilarated to have finally retrieved the horse, though the fate of his uncles simultaneously produced sadness within him. The result was a type of restless melancholy, a sort of emotional twilight. Carrying this unusual feeling within him, he returned to his father's capital. The king was devastated to hear the fate of his sons and eventually died in despair, for he was never able to bring down the Ganga for the benefit of his sixty thousand sons.

After the death of the king, Am-shuman ascended the throne and his son Dileep succeeded him. Both Am-shuman and Dileep lived prosperous and happy lives, yet they both regretted that they were unable to bring the river Ganga down for the benefit of their relations. The son of Dileep was Bhagi-ratha the Valiant, who also desired to bring salvation to his forefathers as well as beget a son.

For this end he entrusted the kingdom to his ministers and went to the Himalayas to practice austerities. King Bhagi-ratha performed severe austerities, called tapasya, by sitting within a ring of fire as well as fasting for long periods of time. This pleased Lord Brahma, the creator of the material universe, who appeared before the king and inquired of his desires.

The king said, "O Lord Brahma, please bless me with your grace! Please allow me to make two requests of you. I pray that you may bless me with a son to carry on the lineage of kings, and also that you order the Ganga to descend to Patala so that the ashes of my ancestors may be purified by her holy waters. Their bodies were burned up due to their offense to Lord Kapila."
Lord Brahma replied, "My dear king, I am very pleased by your austerities and would be happy to grant your requests. However, the Earth cannot stand the force of Ganga's descent. Therefore you must propitiate Lord Shiva, for only he can bear her descending force."

Undaunted, the king renewed his prayers and austerities, this time directing them to the holy feet of Lord Shiva, who oversees the destruction of the universe at the end of each round of material manifestation. Shiva was soon pleased by the prayers, fasting, and selfless intentions of the king. Appearing before him, Lord Shiva spoke as follows: "O king, all good fortune to you. I shall gladly fulfill your desire and receive the Ganges River on my head, for her origin is the holy feet of my worshipful Lord Vishnu, the divine benefactor and maintainer of all."

By the order of Lord Brahma, Ganga began her descent with a tumultuous sound that echoed in all directions. In a haughty mood she thought the force of her waters would sweep Lord Shiva away, but he understood her mood. In order to check her pride, he contained all her waters within the infinite receptacle of his matted locks of hair. For many years she wandered within the maze of Lord Shiva's hair but still could find no outlet.

In the meantime, the king had grown disappointed, for Ganga had still not descended. He again resumed his austerities with such force that Lord Shiva took pity upon him and shook his matted locks, causing some of the Ganga to fall on the place known as Bindu-sarovara. From there the Ganga flowed in seven streams: three to the east, three to the west, and the seventh followed the excited king, who drove his chariot before the great flood of dancing and jumping waters until they flooded and destroyed the ashram of the sage Janu.

The angry Janu was a powerful mystic. By his yogic powers he gathered up the flood of water in his hands and swallowed it all! The demigods and other sages who were present to see the spectacle of the Ganga's descent entreated Janu to release her and allow the king to reap the fruit of his long austerities. This appeased Janu, who released the Ganga. By this incident Ganga also became known as Janavi, the daughter of Janu. Now Ganga flowed unobstructed to Patala, where the king performed the funeral rites for his ancestors, securing for them entrance into the heavenly planets.

After Vishva-mitra had recounted this story, he and the divine brothers Rama and Lakshman took their bath in the waters of the holy Ganga. The scriptures declare that anyone who bathes in the waters of the Ganga, as well as those who read or listen to this narration, shall be cleansed of all sins and filled with virtue. And if one recites the following mantras at the time of bathing, then by the mercy of Ganga, who is a pure devotee of the Lord, one becomes purified in body and mind.

Prayer to Ganga Devi

om vishnu-pada prasutasi
vaishnavi vishnu-pujita   pahi nas tvenasas tasmad
ajanma-maranantikat

"O Ganga-devi, born of Lord Vishnu's holy foot-step, you are honored by Lord
Vishnu Himself as His own energy. Dear mother, please wash away the sins that we
have committed between this birth and death."

tisra-koty ardha-koti cha
tirthanam vayurabravit   divi bhuvyantarikshe cha
tani te shanti jahnavi

"In the heavens and on Earth are situated thirty-five million holy places. O Mother,
all of these are contained within you, and this truth has been
taught by the demigod Vayu."

nandini tyeva te nama
deveshu nalini 'ti cha   vrnda prithvi cha subhaga
vishvakaya shiva sita

"In Devaloka, the world of the demigods, you are called Nandini and Nalini. You are
also known by the names Vrinda,

Prithvi, Subhaga,
Vishvakaya, Shiva and Sita."

vidyadhari suprasana
tatha loka-prasadini   shama cha jahnavi caitanya
shanta shanti-pradayini

"You are also known as Vidyadhari, Suprasana, and Lokaprasadini. O Ksema,
merciful is your name, O Jahnavi and Shanta and Shantipradayini."

etani punya namani
snana-kale prakirtayet   bhavet sanihita atra
ganga tripatha-gamini

"When all these holy names of Ganga are
recited at the time of bathing, then and there the mystic
Ganga appears, who flows in the heavens,
in the sky, and on Earth."

PRAHLAD THE PURE PRINCE

Long ago, at the beginning of the universe, Brahma created the worlds of gods and men through the agency of sound vibration, after having received inspiration and mystic power from Lord Vishnu, the all-pervading Godhead residing within his heart. Marichi was one of the mind-born sons of Brahma, and Marichi's son was Kasyapa. Kasyapa's wife Diti gave birth to two sons named Hiran-yaksha and Hiranya-ka-shipu, as well as a daughter named Simhika.

Hiran-yaksha received boons from Brahma, and as a result became very proud of his prowess as a great hero. Overtaken by pride and arrogance, he destroyed practically everything on the Earth and finally caused the Earth planet to descend to the depths of the universal ocean. It was at that time that Lord Vishnu appeared as Lord Varaha and retrieved the Earth from her submerged condition, thereafter vanquishing Hiran-yaksha in a grand display of martial prowess. All this had been arranged by the inconceivable potency of the Lord, for He desired to exhibit His martial strength and therefore sent His two devotees Jaya and Vijaya to take birth in the world of mortals as Hiran-yaksha and Hiran-ya-kashipu in order that the Lord might have competent adversaries in these pastimes. The two brothers were simply playing the roles of demons but were actually the Lord's own devotees.

The evil king Hiran-ya-kashipu became very angry with Lord Vishnu, desiring to avenge his brother. He decided to perform severe austerities in order to propitiate Brahma. When the evil king left for the forests of Mandara Mountain to begin his yogic practices, the demigods took this opportunity to attack the capital of the demons, hoping to subdue them and thereby stop their unfavorable activities. A great battle ensued and the demons were defeated. The victorious demigods then plundered the palace of the evil king, and it was at this time that the king of the demigods, Indra, captured Kayadhu, the wife of the evil king. The sage Narada felt compassion for her in this distressful condition and, subsequently, convinced Indra to release her to his care by informing him that a great saint would be born of this woman. For some time thereafter, the pregnant Kayadhu stayed in the ashram of Narada and received spiritual instruction from him while engaging in his service. By the mercy and mystic potency of Narada, Kayadhu's unborn child could also hear the spiritual instructions of Narada although still within his mother's womb.

Narada said to Kayadhu, "Dear lady, just as the fruits and flowers of a tree in due course of time undergo the six stages of birth, growth, maintenance, transformation, dwindling, and finally death, the material body, which is acquired by the spirit soul as the result of fruitive activities, similarly undergoes these changes. The spirit soul, however, never undergoes such changes, for it is eternal and inexhaustible. The Supreme Lord and the individual soul are both spiritual and ever free from birth and death. They are not subject to the transformations of matter. The Supreme Lord's unlimited spiritual energies are the source and foundation of all phenomenal manifestations. The individual souls, though eternal, misidentify themselves with the Lord's external energy. As a result they undergo birth and death in material bodies according to the actions and reactions of their desires and material activities."

Narada continued, "The Lord and the individual soul are the conscious witnesses of the body and are never actually affected by the transformations of those bodies. Equipped with these spiritual truths, one should give up the illusory concept of life in which one thinks 'I am this body and everything in relation to this body is mine.' When the intelligence is polluted in this way, one becomes subjugated by the modes of material nature;

thus the soul becomes conditioned by material existence. Just as one may falsely suffer in the dreaming state, in a similar way, due to ignorance, the soul experiences temporary sensations in connection with the body. In truth, everything is the property of the Supreme Lord and should be utilized in His service, for His satisfaction. This process is begun by acceptance of a spiritual master, rendering service to him, and constantly engaging in the glorification of the Lord in the company of affectionate and like-minded seekers. By acting in such devotional consciousness, one can burn up the seeds of fruitive activities and awaken divine love for the Lord." Narada continued to instruct Kayadhu in this way as she engaged in his service there in that beautiful forest ashram.

Meanwhile, in the valley of Mandara Mountain, the evil king was engaged in the severe austerities which he had undertaken for envious material purposes. He thought to himself, "The greatest person in this universe is Brahma, and he has achieved his exalted post by dint of great austerities and mystic power. I too shall perform austerities and become a most powerful person, and then I shall overturn the established order of this world. Everyone will submit to my desires, and I shall become supreme."

Thinking in this way, the evil king stood on his tiptoes for a very great span of time, keeping his arms upward and eyes looking towards the sky. This position was extremely difficult to maintain, yet he accepted it as a means to attain his goal. Because of this terrible austerity the evil king's hair began to emit a glowing effulgence, and fire was seen to blaze from the top of his head which created a disturbing heat throughout the universe. The demigods and all the inhabitants of the worlds became fearful at the sight of this great feat and quickly reported all this to Brahma, hoping that he might take appropriate steps to check this disturbance.

Brahma then proceeded to the place where the evil king stood, accompanied by sages such as Brighu and others. At first Brahma could not see where the evil king was, for the king's body was now covered by an anthill as well as tall grass and bamboo. He had been performing his austerity for one hundred celestial years. One celestial day equals six months of Earth time. Because the evil king had been standing for this great length of time the ants, earthworms, and other parasites had eaten away most of his flesh; therefore he was practically unrecognizable. But because the soul is eternal and exists independently of matter, the evil king was able to maintain himself in that covered condition. He was like a cloud-covered sun, for the whole world could feel the heat of his powerful austerity.

When Brahma saw him he was struck with wonder. Smiling as he sat atop his swanlike conveyance, he said, "O King, please give up these austerities. You are now perfect in this practice, and I wish to grant your desire, whatever it may be. Please tell me what you desire and I shall attempt to fulfill your wish. I am amazed at your endurance and the way you have kept your life air circulating within your bones. Even great saints and sages are unable to perform such severe practices, and therefore let me grant you all the benedictions you seek. I belong to the celestial world of the demigods, who do not die as human beings do, and so my benedictions upon you will not go in vain."

Then Brahma, who is extremely powerful, sprinkled mystic water from his water pot upon the evil king's body which immediately rejuvenated him to the full vigor of youth. The evil king arose from the anthill as an effulgent and renewed man. Seeing Brahma before him in the sky, he offered his respects and said, "O Brahma, best of those who give benedictions, please grant me the boon that I may not meet death from any creature created by you. Please grant me that I may not die either within or outside of any residence, during the day or night, nor on the ground or in the sky. Let me not meet death by any weapon, human being, or animal. Let me not be killed by any demigod or demon. Let me also attain all mystic powers that are obtained by long austerities and yoga practice. Furthermore, please grant me sovereignty over all other beings, and give me the opulence's that are appropriate for that position.

Brahma replied, "O King, these things for which you ask are very difficult to obtain, but in order to award your great austerity I shall now grant you these benedictions. Let it be so." Having blessed the evil king in this way, Brahma, who was very wise, thought within himself that it would be difficult for the evil king to maintain such material achievements. With this in mind the best of the demigods departed for his own planet, Brahma-loka.

Having obtained great powers by the grace of Brahma, the evil king now thought himself to be invincible and once again began to think inimically towards Lord Vishnu, the all-pervading Godhead. He returned to his capital and was later reunited with his wife, who had given birth to their son Prahlad. By his great prowess he subjugated the whole universe and brought everyone except Brahma, Shiva, and Lord Vishnu under his control. Although he was of a cruel nature and his actions were abominable, everyone in the three planetary systems was forced to worship him. In this way he grew more intoxicated by his opulence and power.

The evil king desired to mold his son, Prahlad, according to his own evil and atheistic mentality, thereby making him an instrument to wreak vengeance upon Lord Vishnu. Thinking in this way he entrusted his son to the care of two teachers to be educated in the material sciences of political administration and economics. He also instructed the teachers to never glorify Lord Vishnu or chant His mantra: *om narayanaya namaha*. In fact, he banned the chanting of the holy names of God altogether and instead ordered everyone to glorify him. The prince Prahlad, however, did not like these mundane topics of politics and economics, for political philosophy necessitated seeing others as either friend or enemy, and economics necessitated the exploitation of one group over another. One day as the evil king sat upon his throne in an intoxicated state, he lifted his young son to his lap and inquired affectionately, "What is the best knowledge which you have learned from your teachers?"

The prince replied, "Dear father, those who have accepted a material body are always embarrassed by the anxieties of material life. Therefore one who is truly intelligent should attempt to make a permanent solution to the problems of life by taking shelter of the Divine Godhead Lord Vishnu in devotional service."

Hearing his son glorify Lord Vishnu in this way, the evil king became angry and shouted to the servants, "Who has taught this boy these things? Take him back to the school and be sure that he is properly educated!" The prince was then returned to the care of his two teachers, who tried their best to educate him in worldly affairs by coercion and threats. They feared punishment of the evil king and therefore endeavored very hard to turn the prince's mind away from thoughts of Lord Vishnu and spiritual life.

Some time later the prince was once again brought before his father, who questioned him as to what he had learned from his teachers and what constituted the highest knowledge. To this the prince replied, "Hearing and chanting the holy names of God, remembering Him, serving His divine feet, offering Him worship and prayers, carrying out His orders, considering the Lord to be one's best friend, and surrendering everything to Him—these nine items truly constitute the essence of knowledge, for by such activities one can be relieved of the pains of material existence and achieve devotional love of Godhead, which is the supreme perfection a human being may achieve."

Hearing his son again glorify his enemy Lord Vishnu in this way was like a thunderbolt striking the head of the evil king. With his lips trembling in anger he said to the prince, "You rascal! Where have you received this idea? Surely your teachers have not taught you this!" Standing nearby, the prince's teachers shuddered with fear, anticipating punishment from the evil king, whose eyes burned like red-hot copper balls. They cried out, "No, no, my lord, we have not taught the boy these things!" The enraged king then questioned his son once again: "From whom have you learned about devotional service to Vishnu?" Then the prince indirectly stated that he could not have received true knowledge from his teachers, for they were blind to spiritual truth, being enamored with the objects of this world.

The prince said, "Due to a lack of sense control and addiction to materialistic life, unfortunate persons who are bound by the unrelenting cycle of action and reaction continually chew that which has already been chewed, and gradually progress towards hellish conditions of life. By accepting other persons as their leaders who, like themselves, are bound by material activities, they are continually misdirected towards the external sense objects of this world; and as a result, they fail to recognize that the goal of life is to develop the divine consciousness that will enable one to be eternally engaged in the transcendental loving service of the Lord."

In a fit of rage the evil king threw the boy to the ground and angrily commanded his servants, "Take this boy away from here. He has rejected the values of his family and deserves to be killed! He is engaged in the service of Vishnu, who is our enemy! Remove him at once; I cannot bear the sight of him!"

The servants then seized the boy and, taking him to a dungeon, began to torture him in various ways. Although the servants tried their best to torture and kill the boy, to their amazement he remained unaffected by their actions and spoke to them in this way: "O servants, the all-pervading Lord Vishnu resides in your weapons, within you all, and within me as well. Since this is the truth, your weapons will not injure me." Hearing these words, the servants felt great frustration and angrily threw the saintly boy into a pit of venomous snakes.

The prince, however, remained calm and stood silently meditating on the transcendental form of the Lord despite the repeated bites of the numerous serpents. Indeed, the fangs fell out of the mouths of the snakes! All these wonders took place because Pralad had implicit faith in the protection of the Lord, because he had taken shelter of the divine nature and was therefore protected from adversity. In this connection the scriptures state that all difficulties can be overcome by deeply remembering the Lord:

mac cittah sarva durgani
mat prasadat tarishyasi
atha cet tvam ahankaran
na shroshyasi vinankshyasi

"When you have devoted your heart to Me,
you will be able to surpass all kinds of obstacles and
adversities by My grace. But if out of pride you do not
hear My words, surely you will be lost."

Bhagavad-gita 18.58

Seeing that all the attempts to kill the prince had proved futile, the evil king became a little fearful and began to contrive other means of killing the boy. But after attempting to trample the boy with huge elephants, throwing him from cliffs and into fire, as well as starving the boy and feeding him poison, the prince still remained unaffected! Because he was unsuccessful in all his attempts to subdue the boy, the king who had conquered all the worlds became morose. He could not bear that his desire had been unfulfilled and in frustration sat silently, his head lowered as he thought deeply and wondered how it was that this small boy could remain unaffected by his cruelty. Indeed, the boy appeared to be immortal. This worried the evil king and his servants as well. Then the prince's teachers, along with the palace priests, convinced the evil king to allow them to take the prince back to the school where they would attempt to educate him once again. Reluctantly, the king agreed.

It was not long, however, before the prince began to instruct his classmates when the two teachers were unaware. The prince said, "Dear friends, those who are intelligent should use this valuable human life to practice the spiritual activities of devotional service, wholly abandoning other temporary engagements. Although this material body is temporary, it is very rarely obtained. Therefore it is a most valuable asset in achieving divine love of Godhead, which is the ultimate achievement for all living beings. Complete perfection can be achieved even by the slightest amount of devotional activities. This is also confirmed by the scriptures:

nehabhikrama-nasho 'sti
pratyavayo na vidyate
svalpam apy asya dharmasya
trayate mahato bhayat

"Even a small beginning in devotional service to the Lord cannot go in vain, nor can any loss be suffered. The most insignificant practice of such devotional service saves one from the all-devouring fear of repeated birth and death in this world."

Bhagavad-gita 2.40

The prince continued, "The human form of life is an opportunity for the living entities to reawaken their dormant love of God and return to their spiritual home, in the company of God. This loving

53

devotional reciprocation between the individual soul and the Supreme Soul is a natural condition, because the divine Lord Vishnu is the most beloved of the soul and the supreme well-wisher of all. Moreover, activities, whose sole aim is sense gratification or the attainment of temporary material happiness are actually a waste of time, for everyone automatically obtains happiness, and distress in due course regardless of any endeavors to cultivate such happiness or combat unwanted distress. Therefore, the best use of one's time is to endeavor for the eternal transcendental consciousness of devotional life, which culminates in unending spiritual joy."

After the prince had instructed his classmates in this way, they all took his words very seriously and began to question and reject the materialistic instructions of their teachers, who became fearful seeing the children advance in God consciousness. When news of this new turn of events reached the ears of the evil king, it enraged him. He ordered the prince to be brought before him as he stood trembling with anger he shouted at the boy with words as sharp as razor-tipped arrows.

The evil king screamed, "You impudent little fool! You have disobeyed me for the last time. Until now you have violated my power to rule you. But today I shall send you to the abode of death for your offense of disrupting our family and taking shelter of our enemy! This whole universe is subject to my rule, so I ask you—by whose power do you appear fearless, impudently overstepping my power to rule you?"

The prince was constantly remembering the Lord and, so, was undaunted by his father's anger. In a calm tone of voice he said, "My dear father, the source of my strength as well as your own are the same. Indeed, there is truly only one source of strength, and He is the source of everyone's strength. Whether moving or non-moving, high or low, great or small, everyone is subject to the divine will of God. The Supreme Lord is the source of power of the mind, body, and senses. His influence and power are all-pervading and unlimited. He is the greatest of all and is the ultimate source of this world's creation, maintenance, and final dissolution. O Father, please abandon your discrimination between enemies and friends and be equally disposed towards all beings. In reality, there are no enemies in this world except for the uncontrolled mind. We simply suffer the actions and reactions of our own misdeeds. Enemies are merely imagined by those in ignorance."

The evil king replied, "How dare you minimize my position! I am the supreme controller in this universe, yet you constantly describe a supreme being other than me, who is above everyone and controlling everyone. Where is your God? If He is all-pervading, is He within this pillar? I do not believe in your nonsense ideas about some Supreme God! I am now going to kill you, so let your God save you if He can! I want to see Him!" Speaking thus, the evil king jumped up from his throne with sword in hand and with intense anger struck his fist against the pillar which was nearest to him.

Just then a great sound came from within the column which bewildered the entire assembly. To the amazement of all, the pillar began to crack; as it did so, there arose from within it a most fearful form! It was the Supreme Lord in a form never before seen—appearing with the body of a man and the head of a lion. His brilliant effulgence shone in all directions, illuminating the palace. His eyes were like flaming orbs of anger, and His dagger-like tongue danced within His mouth. He manifested unlimited arms that were equipped with brilliant and fearsome weapons.

The evil king then charged the Lord with his sword and shield and violently attempted to kill Him. But the Lord, whose strength is immeasurable, easily captured the evil king just as the great eagle Garuda captures a snake. While the evil king screamed and wildly shook his limbs, the Lord held him on His lap. Just as the sun was setting, in the twilight, in the doorway of the palace, the Lord tore the demon's chest open with the nails of His beautiful spiritual hands. Exhibiting an extremely frightening countenance, the Lord killed the evil king in such a way that did not interfere with the benedictions of Brahma, who promised that the evil king would not be killed by any weapon, on the earth or in the sky, in either day or night, or by any man or animal.

All the celestial demigods showered flowers from the heavens and began to sing and dance. They were all eager to see this wonderful form of Lord Vishnu. Headed by Brahma and Shiva, they all offered their respectful prayers for the satisfaction of the Lord. They were, however, a bit frightened by the Lord's fierce appearance, so none of them ventured too close to Him. Even Lakshmi, the Goddess of Fortune, who is the Lord's eternal consort, was afraid to approach Him, for even she had never seen this fearsome form of the Lord.

The prince was then requested by Brahma to go forward and try to appease the angry Lord. Thus he hesitatingly approached the Lord and fell down upon the ground to offer his respects, as the Lord looked down in ecstatic affection upon the small boy prostrated at His feet. The Lord then lovingly raised the boy and gently placed His hand upon the prince's head. The instant the prince was touched by the hand of the Lord, he became divinely blessed and began to manifest symptoms of spiritual ecstasy. His eyes welled up with tears, and his heart became over flooded with love for the Lord.

Then, in a voice choked with love, the prince offered this prayer: "O Lord, how is it possible for someone such as myself, who was born in a family of wrongdoers, to offer suitable prayers for Your satisfaction? Even the demigods like Brahma and Shiva are unable to pacify You with their excellent prayers. Then what can be said of me? I am certainly unqualified. Only by sincere devotional service are You satisfied. The possession of wealth, strength, beauty, education, fame, and any other type of opulence is only a disqualification, because all these things create pride in the heart of the possessor; subsequently persons who possess them are often unable to approach You sincerely.

Because You are absolute, any contact with You brings immense spiritual benefit. Therefore I consider that by saving me from the sword of my father, and killing him also, You have spiritually benefited both of us. This is Your mercy upon us, for you are all-good, and Your actions are certainly beneficial for everyone. For myself though, I do not desire any boon other than the opportunity to serve Your devotees, for that is the perfection of life. Those who seek Your favor in order to receive something in trade from You are not pure in their hearts." Speaking in this way, Prahlada offered these and many more sincere and excellent prayers for the glorification of the Lord.

The Lord then replied, "O Prince, may you be blessed with a long life. Without My grace, no one can appreciate or understand Me. But one who has received My favor has nothing more for which to lament or hanker for. Those who are wise seek to please Me alone, for only I can fulfill the desires of everyone." Brahma then said, "My dear Lord, You are the Supreme Soul. If anyone remembers and meditates upon Your spiritual form, You easily protect that person from all types of fear, even the fear of approaching death."

Then, according to the instruction of the Lord, Brahma installed the prince as the new king in his father's place. Prince Pralad duly performed the funeral rites for his deceased father. He then offered his respects to all the assembled demigods according to their respective positions. As they showered their blessings upon him, they all departed for their respective heavenly abodes.

In this way, the two associates of Lord Vishnu, Jaya and Vijaya, who had taken birth as Diti's sons Hiran-yaksha the fighter and the evil king Hiranya-kashipu, were both killed by the Lord. Being illusioned by the Lord's energy, they played the role of evil adversaries but were in reality the Lord's own dear devotees. These same two devotees again took birth as Ravana and Kumba-karna and were vanquished by Lord Rama, the same Personality of Godhead in the role of a great king.

Then they were born a third time as Shishu-pala and Danta-vakra during the pastimes of Lord Krishna 5,000 years ago. Lord Krishna is the original Godhead and source of all, and Lord Vishnu, Lord Rama, and innumerable others are His spiritual expansions, manifested in this world in order to display wonderful pastimes as well as for the upliftment of the materially conditioned souls. As it is described in the scriptures, whenever there is a decline in religion, the Lord personally appears to correct the situation by putting a stop to the activities of the atheists and uplifting the saintly devotees.

yada yada hi dharmasya
glanir bhavati bharata
abhyutthanam adharmasya
tadatmanam srijamy aham

"O Bharata, whenever there is a decline of
religious principles and an uprising
of irreligion, I personally appear
like a being born in this world."

Bhagavad-gita 4.7

By the action of devotional service, pure-hearted devotees who constantly meditate on the Personality of Godhead attain spiritual forms similar to His own. This is described in the scriptures as sarupya-mukti. Although Shishu-pala and Danta-vakra, as well as many others, constantly thought of Lord Krishna as their enemy, still, they achieved the same result, finally returning for good to the unlimited spiritual sky. In that spiritual sky, the Lord is manifested in unlimited spiritual forms on unlimited spiritual planets and engages in unlimited playful loving pastimes with His pure devotees. Such are the mysterious activities of the Lord and His devotees.

etad ya adi-purushasya mrgendra-lilam
daityendra-yutha-pa-vadham prayatah patheta
daityatmajasya ca satam pravarasya punyam
shrutvanubhavam akuto-bhayam eti lokam

"Anyone who attentively hears this holy narration of Lord Nirshinga-deva, the Divine Personality of Godhead, and His pure devotee Pralad Maharaja, will surely reach the spiritual world, which is ever free from fear."

Srimad Bhagavatam 7.10.47

HIGH THOUGHTS

By the edge of a forest there lived a brahmin. Though very poor, his mind was composed. Even in the face of adverse circumstances he remained calm and equipoised, believing that man must suffer or enjoy the consequences of his own karma. Once while in the assembly of saintly persons this simple brahmin heard that personal service to saints is always preferable, though in the absence of such personal service one can also practice devotion even with one's inner thoughts.

Because the brahmin was poor and could not afford expensive paraphernalia for the Lord's worship, he began to practice this method of mental devotional service. He would take his daily bath in the river and afterwards be seated in a solitary place. By the practice of breath control he would calm his mind and thereafter mentally install the deity of Lord Vishnu in his heart. Thinking himself to be wearing clean cloth, he would prostrate himself before the Lord and, after mentally collecting water from the Ganga and Yamuna Rivers, he would bathe the Lord with those holy waters, pouring them from gold and silver pitchers. Next he would mentally offer the Lord delicious foods and other beautiful ingredients of worship, such as tulasi buds, fragrant flower garlands, incense and ghee lamps. Then he would offer some water in a conchshell, fan the Lord with a whisk fan and end his worship by mentally sounding the conch shell horn.

After many years of such mental worship of the Lord, the poor brahmin one day prepared payesa, a mixture of rice, sugar and milk. In his mind he poured the sweet rice onto a golden plate but, before offering it to the Lord, thought to check its temperature so he dipped his finger in the hot preparation—and felt it burn his finger! He then thought to himself that the sweet rice had become unholy by his touching it—and that it was therefore unofferable to the Lord. Being pained by this thought, his meditation was broken. When he opened his eyes he saw to his great astonishment that his physical finger was actually burned!

At this, Lord Vishnu in Vaikuntha smiled. Seeing the Lord's beautiful smile, Lakshmi was surprised and curious as to why the Lord had smiled. When she asked her Lord the reason, He sent a celestial chariot and brought the devoted brahmin to Vaikuntha and told Lakshmi all about him. Thereafter He blessed the brahmin with an eternal seat by the side of the Lord Himself.

In the sacred book of devotion Bhakti-rasamrta-sindhu, the author Srila Rupa Goswami has cited the following verse in connection with *seva-dhyanam*, or meditation on the services of the Lord:

> manasenopacarena, paricarya harim sada
> pare vanmanasa gamyam, tam sakshat pratipedire

> "By constantly serving the Lord with mind-created ingredients of service, some devotees have attained in person that Supreme Lord who is beyond all mundane expressions and the mental grasp of the imagination."

Bhakti-rasamrta-sindhu 2.182

THE TALE OF JADA

From the ancient scripture known as the Vishnu Purana we learn that thousands of years ago in the land of Hima there lived a pious king named Nabi with his wife, Meru, and son, Rishab. When Rishab became king he fathered one hundred sons, the oldest of which was named Bharat.

After Rishab had passed away, Bharat ascended the throne and ruled the kingdom with his wife, Pancha. They had five sons. It is from this righteous King Bharat that India got its name Bharata-varsha, having formerly been known as Ajanabha-varsha. Like his father before him, Bharat was very learned in the scriptures, affectionate, and respectful of the brahmins. Though expertly engaged in his kingly duties, he constantly meditated upon the shining param-atma within his heart. This param-atma is the all-pervading plenary expansion of the Personality of Godhead, the indwelling spiritual controller and witness of all things.

Bharat righteously ruled the country in this way for many years before retiring and subsequently dividing his kingdom among his sons. Desiring to free himself from the entanglement of worldly life and awaken spiritual love for God in his heart, the king renounced his royal opulence and took up residence in the forest at the ashram of the great sage Pulaha.

There was a beautiful river flowing in front of the ashram that was called chakra-nabhi, so named because on one side of the river the rocks had marks of a chakra (disc), and on the other side there were marks of a nabhi (navel). This river is also known as the Gandaki, and from within this river come the sacred shaligrama-shila stones. That riverside ashram was located near present-day Haridwar.

In the gardens of Pulaha-ashrama the king lived alone and collected from the forest lovely flowers and tulasi leaves. He also collected water from the Gandaki River and fruits, roots, and bulbs which he offered in worship to the Lord. In this way he became peaceful and lived a simple life sanctified by pure devotional activities. In time his devotional meditation and puja intensified by constant practice and, as he became more absorbed in the service of the Lord, his attraction for worldly life diminished. He performed strict austerities and many other types of ritual and devotional activities, and in this way worshiped by offering the results of all his activities unto the Lord.

Every morning the king would bathe in the river, after which he would chant the sacred gayatri mantra. One day as he was just finishing his bath, a thirsty, pregnant doe came to drink at the side of the river. Just as she bent her head to drink, the loud roar of a lion came from the forest nearby. Frightened, the deer jumped into the river to cross. As a result, the doe gave birth unexpectedly. The baby deer that was born at that moment began to float downstream, all the while crying piteously. The king witnessed all this and, being compassionate by nature, felt concern for the fawn and ran to rescue it. He recovered the fawn from the river and brought it to his ashram with the intention of returning it to its mother, but later he found the mother deer lying dead in a nearby cave.

Feeling pity for this beautiful and helpless creature, the king's mind was increasingly diverted from his spiritual practices. He began to affectionately take care of the young deer, who would follow him everywhere. Soon the bond of affection between the king and the deer had grown very strong. If the deer did not return from grazing at the usual time, the king would become very concerned and go searching through the forest for his missing pet.

After many years had passed the king eventually became old, and the time of death approached him. On the day of his destined passing, he was anxiously searching for the deer and fell to his death from a mountainside. The mind of the king was absorbed in thoughts of the deer as he left his material body. As a result he acquired the body of a deer in his next life, although by dint of his devotional practices he was able to remember all the incidents of his former life as King Bharat. This great mystery of how the eternal soul transmigrates from one body to another is clearly described in the scriptures:

yam yam vapi smaran bhavam
tyajaty ante kalevaram
tam tam evaiti kaunteya
sada tad-bhava-bhavitah

"O son of Kunti, at the time of leaving the body, whatever form a person meditates upon will be attained by him, due to his constant contemplation on that form."

Bhagavad-gita 8.6

Though now situated in the body of a deer, the king was fully cognizant of what had taken place and greatly lamented his misfortune, by internally repenting and praying to the Lord. Realizing the seriousness of his situation, he immediately left the family of deer he had been born into and returned to his former ashram. Upon his arrival at his former residence he remained quietly in the form of a deer and lived on dry leaves until the death of that body.

The king next took birth as the son of a learned brahmin in the dynasty of Angira. His father had two wives: the first begot nine sons, and by his second wife he begot twins—a boy and girl, the male child being the king himself. He was now known as Jada.

By dint of his previous devotional yoga practices he could clearly remember the incidents of his former lives. Although he had once again received the body of a human being, he greatly feared the possibility of another fall down. So, in order to protect himself, he presented himself to others as a madman, pretending to be deaf and dumb so that others would not distract him from his constant meditation on the spiritual form of the Lord.

Jada's father was very affectionate to him and tried his best to teach him the lessons of Vedic knowledge, but Jada purposely behaved like a fool. Eventually Jada's father passed away without ever being successful in the education of his son. When Jada's mother passed away shortly thereafter, her two children were left in the care of her elder co-wife. The nine stepbrothers of Jada abandoned all attempts to educate him, considering him to be dull and brainless.

These ignorant stepbrothers had no knowledge of spiritual matters and consequently could not recognize Jada's exalted spiritual status. Erroneously thinking that fruitive activities were the only goal of life, they became degraded by cruel behavior and horribly mistreated Jada, who never protested even though he was fully aware of their harsh treatment. They treated him as if he were nothing more than a beast of burden by insulting him and feeding him rejected and stale foodstuffs.

Jada wore only a loincloth and a sacred thread and was covered with dirt because he slept on the ground, never caring to cover or clean himself. Because his body was dirty, his spiritual radiance and knowledge remained covered, just like a valuable gemstone that is covered by dirt.

Although he was spiritually advanced, the local people considered him retarded and repeatedly insulted him as he wandered here and there. This did not affect him, however, because he was completely aloof from the dualities of material happiness and distress. His only concern was to finish his involvement with the material world and enter the spiritual domain of God.

One dark night Jada's stepbrothers ordered him to watch over their grain fields. Nearby, the leader of the local dacoits (murderous outlaws), who was desirous of obtaining a son, had captured a man and was leading him to be sacrificed to the goddess Kali. Low class men such as these are overpowered by ignorance and, as a result, sometimes concoct such abominable worship of demigods like Kali in order to fulfill their material desires.

To achieve these ends they would sometimes make a human sacrifice of a dull man to propitiate the deity. Along the way, however, the man who was to be sacrificed had escaped. The disappointed dacoits were roaming about the night in search of a substitute when they came upon Jada, who was sitting and watching over the fields. Thinking him to be an excellent choice for their sacrifice, the dacoits immediately bound Jada and led him with delight to the temple of goddess Kali.

According to the rituals of their sacrifice, the dacoits dressed Jada in fine garments and fed him sumptuously. Then, adorning him with oils, sandalwood pulp and garlands, they offered incense and flowers to the deity while singing prayers and songs to the accompaniment of musical instruments. After this worship of the goddess had gone on for some time, one of the dacoits, who was acting as the priest, prepared to offer the blood of Jada to the goddess.

Taking up a large sword and consecrating it with the mantra of Kali, he raised it to kill Jada. Jada, however, remained unaffected by this dangerous situation. Being materially indifferent, he sat silently thinking of the Lord within his heart. Because he was fully surrendered to the Personality of Godhead, he had no fear. This fearless condition of the Lord's fully surrendered devotees is described by Lord Shiva:

narayana para sarve
na kutashcana bibyati
svargapavarga narakeshev
api tulyartha-darshinah

"Those devotees who are fully surrendered in the devotional
service of the Supreme Lord Narayana (Vishnu) are never
fearful of any adverse condition of life. Such devotees are
exclusively interested in the Lord's service, and therefore
consider the positions of heaven, hell, and liberation to
be equally insignificant."

Srimad-Bhagavatam 6.17.28

Jada Bharat was a saint of the highest order, and to harm such a
person is the greatest sin. The goddess Kali herself is a devotee
of Lord Vishnu, as are all the demigods who have received their
delegated powers from Him. Therefore she could not bear to
let these rogues carry out such a heinous atrocity in her name.
Suddenly the deity form of the goddess burst apart, and the
blazingly effulgent form of goddess Kali personally emerged from
it. Taking up the sword that the dacoits had intended to kill Jada
with, she immediately slew the rogues. It is actually the function
of goddess Kali to kill all demoniac elements in the world, but
the foolish dacoits did not realize this and were subsequently
punished for their offense.

Jada was a pure devotee of the Lord and, so, remained unharmed
by the grace of the furious goddess, who considers it her duty to
protect the saintly and destroy the wicked. Being fully absorbed
in the spiritual knowledge that distinguishes the eternal self from
matter, Jada was not the least bit disturbed, even in the face of
such great provocation. This is the nature of great saints who

regard friend and foe equally and, as a result, are fully protected by the Lord.

Soon after this incident, Jada began wandering near a great river. At that time, apparently by coincidence, King Rahu-gana, the ruler of the states of Sindhu, was passing by in his palanquin. As the king's palanquin carriers reached the shore of the river, they realized they needed another carrier. Seeing the stout-bodied Jada nearby, they immediately enlisted him in this service. But due to Jada's sense of nonviolence, he carried the palanquin very erratically—for, as he walked forward, he was very careful not to step on any ants. Thus he could not walk in time with the other carriers, who became fearful because the king began to chastise them.

The carriers told the king: "O lord, we are not neglecting our duty in carrying your palanquin properly. The cause of this disturbance is this new man who has been recently engaged in your service. He cannot walk properly. As a result the palanquin is shaking." Being intelligent, the king could immediately understand the situation. The king, however, was easily angered and began to sarcastically criticize Jada as if he were weak and feeble. Jada was unaffected by the harsh words of the king and remained silent, absorbed in the ecstasy of spiritual realization within himself, and continued to carry the palanquin as before. This enraged the king, who began threatening and severely chastising Jada, who still remained unaffected due to his complete identification with spirit.

Jada always carried the divine form of the Lord within his heart, and was a kind well-wisher to all living beings. He did not maintain any bodily conception of himself, for he was fully absorbed in the subjective nature of the self. Therefore, despite being insulted by the king, he sweetly smiled and humbly said, "Your criticism of me is just appropriate, coming from one who is ignorant of the progressive spiritual values of life. Actually, I am not this physical body, and therefore your sarcastic statements that I am not physically strong are indeed correct. Presently you are considering yourself to be a king and that I am your servant, yet all these bodily designations are temporary and have no bearing whatsoever on the soul. Today you are king and I your servant, but tomorrow these positions may be changed, and you may become the servant and I your master. If you persist in your erroneous conception that you are a king and I am your servant, then please order me, and I shall obey your command."

Being a learned man, the king could at once recognize the spiritually potent philosophical words of Jada as that which is approved by all scriptural authorities. Realizing that he had offended a great soul, the king immediately alighted from his palanquin and fell flat at the feet of Jada, seeking the saint's pardon for his disgraceful conduct. The king said, "Please forgive my insulting behavior. It appears that you are moving in this world in a covered way, and therefore your exalted spiritual stature is unrecognizable to others. You must be a highly advanced liberated saint, whose mission it is to do good to others. Please therefore instruct me."

Jada said, "As long as the mind remains contaminated by ignorance, it behaves like an uncontrolled elephant. It seeks to expand the field of material activities through the agency of the senses, and thus it binds the eternal soul to the material world in order to enjoy or suffer the karmic reactions of material activities. "The eleven bodily senses and the five great elements (earth, water, fire, air, ether) constitute a total of sixteen material elements, all of which are grouped about the mind.

When the mind of the eternal living soul is situated in either a higher or lower position, the soul takes a corresponding birth in a higher or lower body amongst the demigods, human beings or animals. In this way, the materialistic mind carries the eternal soul to different species of life to taste the illusion of material sorrow and happiness. However, when the mind becomes detached from sense objects and takes shelter of the spiritual service of God, that very same mind becomes the cause of liberation.

"The Supreme Lord is all-pervading in His feature as the oversoul, or param-atma and is known as Vishnu. He is spiritually self-satisfied and the cause of all creation. If He chooses to do so, He can reveal Himself through the agency of divine sound, for He is always fully independent of the six transformations of the material energy (birth, growth, maintenance, production of by-products, dwindling and death). As Vishnu He is the shelter and resting place of all spiritual and material energies." In this way Jada instructed the king in the science of spiritual knowledge, and by speaking the following verse he revealed the way to properly attain the mercy of the Lord:

> rahuganaitat tapasa na yati
> na chejyaya nirvapanad grhad va
> na chandasa naiva jalagni-suryair
> vina mahat-pada-rajo-'bhishekam

"My dear king, unless one has the opportunity to anoint his body with the dust of the lotus feet of great saints, one cannot realize the Absolute Truth. That Absolute Truth is not realized by observing celibacy, by worshiping the deity, by renunciation, or by perfectly following the rules of married life. Nor can one attain the truth by accepting severe penances and austerities, by studying the Vedas, nor by performing ritualistic ceremonies. Only by taking shelter of a fully dedicated servant of the Lord can one realize the Absolute Truth."

Srimad-Bhagavatam 5.12.12

UNLIKELY FRIENDS

Long ago, there lived a man named Bima who lived by cheating and stealing. He was a man of bad character who had killed many brahmins and enjoyed the wives of other men. He made his living by robbing others of their wealth, and once, with a plan of robbery in mind, he approached the house of a brahmin and stood at the doorstep speaking in a pathetic tone. He said, "O respectable sir, please hear my grievance. As you are a kindhearted brahmin, please be compassionate and give me some rice, for I am very hungry and will surely die without food."

The brahmin replied, "Dear hungry guest, there is no one here to cook for you, but I shall give you some rice that you may cook for yourself daily and thereby regain your strength. I have no father or mother, nor do I have a wife, a son, or a brother. Indeed, I am living here alone without the company of relatives. All of them are now dead and gone." Bima said, "O revered brahmin, I too am a lonely person. Please permit me to stay here as your servant." The words of Bima so touched the brahmin that he immediately cooked some rice and served it to Bima.

From that day on Bima remained with the brahmin as his servant, all the while waiting for some convenient moment to rob him and run away. But since Bima would daily wash the brahmin's feet and take that water on his head, he gradually became purified of his evil intentions, and actually began to serve the brahmin with sincere devotion. This miraculous change of heart came about due to the internal purity of the brahmin, who was a shudha-bhakta, a pure devotee of the Lord.

One night, another thief broke into the brahmin's room to steal his gold earrings. Bima was awakened by the thief's movements and rushed forward to beat him and drive him away, but in the darkness Bima could not see the sword in the hand of this thief. With one heavy blow the thief cut off Bima's head, and quickly escaped through the window. Just then, Bima found himself in a beautiful, airy subtle form, separate and distinct from the gross physical body which lay bleeding before him. As he remained there, in astonishment he saw a mysteriously beautiful light descending from above. As the light drew closer he could make out the inconceivably beautiful angelic forms of the attendants of Lord Vishnu, who had come to lead him in his spiritual form to the eternal spiritual sky.

A divine chariot appeared that was drawn by splendidly large, beautiful, and regal-looking swans, and Bima stepped into that magnificent conveyance and was taken up to the spiritual sky. Though he lost his gross physical form, he achieved a siddha-swarupa, a perfect spiritual form, because he died nobly in the service of a pure devotee of the Lord. The scriptures confirm that service rendered to saintly persons gives one the greatest fortune:

sadhu-sanga, sadhu-sanga
sarva-shastre kaya
lava-matra sadhu-sange
sarva-siddhi haya

"The verdict of all the revealed scriptures is that by serving a saint even for one moment, one can attain all success."

Chaitanya-Charitamrita M.22.54

SEARCH FOR THE GREATEST

Long, long ago all the great sages gathered together to perform a grand religious observance on the banks of a holy river. Soon a dispute arose among them as to who was the greatest of the three presiding deities. Some of the sages were inclined towards Lord Brahma, others declared that Lord Vishnu is the greatest, and still others asserted the superiority of Lord Shiva.

After much debate they unanimously elected the sage Brighu to ascertain the truth of the matter, and he soon began his journey to the celestial planets. Brighu first arrived at the assembly of Lord Brahma. In an apparently disrespectful manner, he entered the assembly and took his seat amongst the other sages gathered there without offering any respect to Brahma. Brahma was visibly annoyed by this act of disrespect, and Brighu quickly left for Mount Kailas, the abode of Lord Shiva.

Upon seeing the sage's arrival at Kailas, Lord Shiva rose from his seat and approached him to embrace and welcome him. But when the sage shrank back, crying out, "Don't touch me!", Shiva became furious and was about to hit him with his trident when Parvati stopped him. Leaving Kailas, the sage next traveled to the spiritual abode of Lord Vishnu. There he saw the maintainer of the universe resting on His divine serpent-bed Ananta absorbed in spiritual slumber.

Finding Vishnu in slumber, the sage gave a hard kick to the chest of the Lord. Springing up suddenly, Lord Vishnu saw the sage standing before Him and begged the sage to pardon Him for His disrespect, inquiring if the sage's foot was in pain after contacting His hard chest. With remarkable humility the Lord solemnly declared that He would always carry sage's footprint on His chest as a sign of repentance for having shown disrespect to the sage. This footprint still remains on the chest of Lord Vishnu and is known as shrivatsa. The sage was astonished to see the behavior of the Lord and therefore concluded that Lord Vishnu is certainly the greatest of all. Visvambar visvera kalyana: "The all-good is the maintainer of the universe, and it is through affection that He is so." The Bhagavad-gita has confirmed this truth:

bhoktaram yajna tapasam
sarva loka maheshvaram
suridam sarva bhutanam
jnatva mam shantim richati

"I am the enjoyer of the results of all sacrifices and austerities performed by the fruitive workers and liberation-seekers. I am the only proprietor and controller of all planes of life, and I am the most adored friend and well wisher of all. The soul who thus knows My true identity attains the ecstasy of knowing his own divine identity."

Bhagavad-gita 5.29

THE SECRET MANTRA

Rama-nuja was a South Indian brahmin who traveled and taught throughout India, and during his lifetime of 120 years he wrote major commentaries on the Vedas, the Vedanta-sutras, and the Bhagavad-gita. Rama-nuja taught the vasishta-dvaita philosophy of qualified non-dualism, which is a form of personal theism. He defeated the monistic ideology by scripturally proving that there is a difference between the Supreme Soul and the individual souls, and that they are eternally related through loving devotion, bhakti.

After the passing of Yamun-acharya, Rama-nuja became the acharya or leader of the Shri sampradaya. Rama-nuja was born on the fifth day of the full moon in the Vedic month of Chaitra in 1017 A.D. and established himself as a great scholar at an early age. He took great personal risks for the spiritual benefit of others, and this is illustrated by the following story.

There once was an Alwar (South Indian guru) named Goshti-purna, who had the highest type of mantra. Rama-nuja approached the Alwar to receive initiation into that mantra but was refused, for the Alwar was reluctant to give such a confidential mantra to a relative newcomer. Rama-nuja approached the Alwar eighteen times with great respect and humility, finally breaking into tears and pleading for his mercy. At last the Alwar decided to give him the mantra after first swearing him to absolute secrecy. The Alwar told Rama-nuja, "If you promise not to disclose this mantra to anyone, then I shall reveal it to you." Rama-nuja agreed, and with this pledge received the mantra.

The Alwar then whispered the mantra into Rama-nuja's ear, saying, "This mantra is most powerful. Whoever chants it will obtain liberation; he will enter the spiritual planets where he will achieve the personal service of the Lord." As Rama-nuja left the temple, a crowd gathered around him. It had been announced to the public that Rama-nuja was receiving that special mantra, and thus many people were standing outside waiting. Immediately the crowd began to impatiently ask him, "What kind of mantra has the Alwar given you? What is the mantra? Is it of the highest type, one that will deliver us all?" Inspired to distribute the wonderful mantra that would free anyone who chanted it from material existence, Rama-nuja announced to the crowd, "Please chant this mantra:

"Om namo narayanaya."

The crowd was overjoyed and felt that they had been truly blessed, but when the news reached the Alwar, he called Rama-nuja back. Outraged that his new disciple would disobey his order so quickly, he demanded an explanation. "You promised to keep the mantra a secret. Why have you indiscriminately revealed it to all those people? Do you understand the penalty for such misbehavior?" Rama-nuja replied, "Yes, I understand the consequences of my actions: I may go to hell for disobeying your order."

"Then why have you done this?" his guru asked. Rama-nuja replied, "Dear master, I realized that the power of the mantra you gave me could deliver everyone who hears it. Seeing the earnest desire of the crowd to be saved from material life, I felt some divine inspiration to distribute your mercy to them. If this is a sin, then I must be punished. If my sin warrants it, you may condemn me to hell. But please spare those innocent people from your wrath." Hearing the sincerity of his disciple, the Alwar's heart was moved. After all, what greater principle can there be than the distribution of the Lord's mercy?

Although Rama-nuja had apparently disobeyed the formal letter of his guru's instructions regarding the mantra, he had in fact understood the real spirit of the mantra itself. If anyone can take this sort of risk, their guru will bless them, and they cannot be doomed. On the basis of genuine spiritual inspiration, devoid of personal interest, a disciple may take that sort of risk for the benefit of others.

Wherever there is the eye of the Lord, the Supreme Guru, one cannot but be saved. Another great indian saint by the name of Jiva Goswami has written: *jnana shat ya vittha shat ya:* "If I have some money and another person is suffering with no money—if I hang on tightly to my money and my neighbor lies fasting without food, then I'll be responsible for his suffering. So if I have some knowledge, if I can help my neighbor, but don't do that, I'll be responsible. By not helping him, I commit an offense against society." The Srimad-Bhagavatam gives this recommendation:

etavaj janma-saphalyam
dehinam iha dehishu
pranair arthair diya vaca
shreya-acharanam sada

"It is the duty of every living being to perform
welfare activities for the benefit of others with
his life, wealth, intelligence, and words."

Srimad-Bhagavatam 10.22.35

A GOOD EXAMPLE

Rama-nuja had a disciple named Danur-das who was very attached to his beautiful wife. One day, Rama-nuja asked him if he wanted to see real beauty, and out of curiosity Danur-das agreed. Rama-nuja then took him to the temple of Lord Vishnu and asked him to behold the beauty of the deity. Upon realizing that the Lord's spiritual beauty eclipses all the beauties of this world, Danur-das increasingly became a great devotee follower of Rama-nuja.

By dint of his strong mood of service towards his master Rama-nuja, Danur-das soon became quite detached from material objects. To teach detachment to one of his other disciples, Rama-nuja once staged the following demonstration: he told this disciple to go to the place where the renounced mendicant priests bathe and switch their clothing around, so that after bathing there would be some confusion. When the priests—who were all renowned scholars and renunciates—were finished bathing, they found that their clothes had been mixed up. One priest was wearing the cloth of another, and so an argument ensued. As one after another finished his bath and went to find his clothes, the argument grew more heated. In this way, these great masters of renunciation were seen to be attached to some pieces of old cloth.

Then Rama-nuja sent his disciple to the home of Danur-das after first arranging for Danur-das to do some service in the temple, thus making sure that he would not be at home. The disciple went to the home of Danur-das in the evening, and following the order of Rama-nuja, began stealing the jewelry from the body of Danur-das's wife as she slept. After stripping the ornaments from one side of her body, he was about to go when suddenly she turned over in her sleep. The disciple was startled and left through the window immediately. Rama-nuja had instructed him to wait outside the window for the return of Danur-das, and to note his reaction.

After some time Danur-das returned home, and his wife asked him, "Danur-das, is there something wrong at the temple?"

"No, my dear," Danur-das replied. "Why?"
"I am worried that they are in need of money but are ashamed to ask for it. We must do something to help them."
"What makes you say that?"

"Because one of the devotees from the temple silently entered in through the window while I was lying in bed, and thinking that I was asleep, began taking the jewelry from my body. I think those poor saints must desperately need our help to do something like that."

"What did you do?"
"I turned over, and he fled through the window."
"Why did you do that? You scared him away!"

"I didn't mean to scare him. I only turned over so that he could take the ornaments from the other side of my body as well."
Danur-das chastised her, saying, "If you were not so affected by false ego, you would have stopped him and given him all your jewels. Now what will we do? We have failed miserably!" Hearing this his wife began to lament, saying, "You are right. It is only my selfishness that kept me from surrendering everything. How will I ever make any advancement?"

From his hiding place Rama-nuja's disciple was astonished at the humility and surrender of Danur-das and his chaste wife. When he returned to his guru, he reported everything that had taken place.

Rama-nuja then explained the meaning of both of the events which his disciple had witnessed: the priests were so attached to some ragged bits of cloth that they were fighting over them, whereas Danur-das and his wife, although householders, were so free from attachment to material things that they were ready to have their jewels stolen by the devotees if they were needed for the service of the Lord.

In this way Rama-nuja very expertly taught his disciples through example as well as precept that only when one recognizes the supreme proprietorship of the Lord can one truly become peaceful, as is nicely described in the Bhagavad-gita:

> vihaya kaman ya sarvan
> pumams carati nih sprha
> nirmamo nirahankarah
> sa shantim adhigacchati

"Giving up all kinds of sensual desires, unattached to the objects of the senses, free from false ego and a false sense of possessiveness, certainly such a person attains tranquility, having reawakened one's divine relationship with the Absolute Truth."

Bhagavad-gita 2.71

THE VIRTUOUS KING

Once, in a great and beautiful city of ancient India, a poor man approached the king, who was famous as the most truthful and virtuous. He asked the king for some help, and the king said, "Come tomorrow, and I will give you what you want."

The king's brother overheard this and ran at once to the place where a great bell was hanging, and which was rung only on the occasion of a special event or victory. The brother immediately began to ring the bell. The people became excited to suddenly hear the bell and came from all directions to ascertain what great deed or victory had taken place. The king was also surprised when he heard that his brother had rung the bell, and he called for him to come to the royal hall to give an explanation.

When questioned by the king, the brother replied, "We have gained a great victory today—victory over death for twenty-four hours. You, my king, have asked that man to return tomorrow, saying you would then give him what he wanted. And that means that until tomorrow, you, who are truth and virtue personified are not going to die, which is indeed a triumph over death. This is a great victory."

The king was astonished. He immediately called the poor man back to the palace and gave him what he desired without waiting for the next day. Some time later in the forest, the king's father Yama-raj asked his royal son, "What is the most wonderful thing in this world?" The king 's remarkable reply was:

ahany ahani bhutani
gacchantiha yamalayam
sheshah stavaram icchanti
kim ashcaryam atah param

"Every day, hundreds and millions of living beings go to the kingdom of death. Still, those who remain living forget that death may take them away at any time. What could be more wonderful than this?"

Mahabharata, Vana. 313.116

SERVING THE WISE

There once was a simple and gentle man named Das. He was a humble devotee of Lord Vishnu. Though married for many years, he had not been blessed with a child in spite of all the austerities and rituals performed by him for this purpose.

One day, the great sage Narada happened to pass through the village where Das lived. Greeting the sage with humility and respect, Das inquired where the sage was going. The sage replied that he was on his way to the spiritual abode of Lord Vishnu. The sage was such an advanced saint that he could travel anywhere in the spiritual or material worlds by the power of his mystic potency. Upon hearing this, Das anxiously requested the sage to inquire of Lord Vishnu as to why He had not yet blessed him with a child, and when he might expect to have that blessing.

Upon leaving Das, the sage quickly ascended to the spiritual sky by the power of his mystic potency. When he reached the spiritual planet of Lord Vishnu he found the Lord in the company of His eternal consort Lakshmi, the goddess of fortune. They were sitting on a beautiful golden throne in a magnificent garden surrounded by lush trees and clear ponds, where snow white swans swam among pink lotus blossoms. The divine couple shone with a soft brilliance that was brighter than the sun, yet cooler than the rays of a full autumn moon. They greeted the sage with smiling affection, and after offering him a comfortable seat, inquired as to the purpose of his visit. the sage related to Lord Vishnu the query of the devoted Das, and the Lord replied that Das was not destined to have a child in this life.

The sage did not wish to communicate this unpleasant news to Das. Therefore, many years passed before the sage again saw him in the village. At that time when the sage finally entered Das's house once again, he saw three children playing in the courtyard and was astonished to learn that they belonged to Das. The sage was naturally curious to hear how Das had come to have these beautiful children, and he then made inquires of him. Das replied that since his last meeting with the sage, a wonderful thing had occurred. He had met another saint and was able to render him some service. The saint was pleased with the service rendered by Das, and instructed him to renounce his solitary austerities and ritualistic worship that was materially motivated for the birth of a child. Out of compassion the saint then blessed him saying that he would have not one but three children. Soon afterwards the wife of Das gave birth to her first of three children. Das then realized he had been foolish, and began to serve the saint with sincere earnestness, no longer performing religious activities for material results.

Hearing this, the sage Narada quickly set out once again for the spiritual sky, astonished that the word of Lord Vishnu had not come true. Upon reaching Lord Vishnu's spiritual planet, the sage inquired, "My Lord, several years ago I spoke to You about a devotee whom You said was not destined to have a child, yet now I find that he has three children." Lord Vishnu then laughed in a way that resembled the rumbling of thunderclouds, and smiling at Lakshmi, said, "That must be the work of some saint, for the saints are so wonderful that they can change one's destiny." Because Das had been eager to learn about spiritual life while in the service of a saintly person, not only were his spiritual aspirations fulfilled, but his material desires as well.

This is merely a by-product of living a life based on higher principles.

akamah sarva kamo va
moksha-kama udara dhih
tivrena bhakti yogena
yajeta purusham param

"A person with broader intelligence, who may be filled with material desires, or may be freed from material desires, who also desires liberation, by all means must worship and serve the Absolute Truth."

Srimad-Bhagavatam 2.3.10

HEART OVER HEAD

There once was a young man who aspired for God-realization. He wanted to know how he could best know and understand the Absolute Truth. One day as he sat beneath a tree on the bank of a beautiful river, the holy sage Narada happened to pass by. Seeing the great saint, the boy immediately showed him respect and inquired of him how he might attain spiritual perfection.

The sage pointed to the boy's reflection on the surface of the water and said, "Your material body is like the image on the water: ever changing with the flow of time. Just as you stand here on the shore unaffected, in reality you are an eternal soul, actually unaffected by birth and death, yet your consciousness is illuminating and reflecting upon the temporary forms of this world. Dive deep into reality," said the sage, "by constantly repeating and remembering the holy names of the Lord. This will awaken divine love in your heart for the Supreme Godhead." Then the sage wished him well and departed.

Although the young man felt the sage's analogy concerning the soul was profound, he had no faith in the power of God's names. He had the idea that one should learn Sanskrit and master the Vedas before one could have God-realization. Disregarding the advice of the sage, he went to a teacher who was well versed in the Vedas and other scriptures and requested that he teach him Sanskrit.

The teacher agreed, but added that the young man should do some service besides the engagement of his studies. The young man was given the job of tending the cows of the ashram, and whenever he had spare time, he went to the teacher to receive his lessons in Sanskrit. After eleven years had passed the young man had grown mature, and had become a great Sanskrit scholar with good knowledge of the Vedas and other shastras or scriptures. Yet in spite of his vast learning he still did not realize God. He then asked his teacher why he had not attained God consciousness, even though he was now learned in all the scriptures.

His teacher then told him that mere scholarship and knowledge did not lead to God-realization. "To realize God, one must love Him intensely by serving His saintly devotees, and constantly remember Him by repeating His holy names. Devotion is always above knowledge," he said. Surprised by the statement of his teacher, the student realized his mistake in disregarding the advice of the sage Narada, who had requested him to practice remembrance of the names of God eleven years before.

He regretted that he had wasted many precious years in study without chanting God's names. He realized that knowledge is a dry thing which only engages the mind, whereas only love and devotion to God can quench the thirst of the heart. At that time he recalled from the scriptures a verse spoken by a great saintly king:

tarko 'pratishtah shrutayo vibhinna
rishir yasya matam na bhinnam
dharmasya tattvam nihitam guhayam
mahajano yena gatah sa panthah

"Dry arguments are inconclusive. Simply by studying the Vedas, which are variegated, one cannot come to the right path by which religious principles are understood. The solid truth of religious principles is hidden in the heart of an unadulterated self-realized person. Consequently, as the scriptures confirm, one should accept whatever progressive path the saints advocate."

Mahabharata, Vana-parva 313.117

THE HOLY NAME

The famous sage Narada was a great devotee of the Lord's holy name. He repeated the holy name of God and traveled all over the world proclaiming its greatness twenty-four hours a day. At one time he became a little proud of his continuous chanting because he saw that most people would only chant the name for a short time during the day, whereas he was chanting all day and night. As a result he considered himself to be the Lord's greatest devotee.

In the course of his wanderings he visited the unlimited spiritual abode of Lord Vishnu. Seeing the face of Narada, Lord Vishnu could understand that he had become proud of his devotion. The sage, with an air of self-importance, asked Lord Vishnu who His greatest devotee was. With a smile as beautiful and pleasing as a sweetly scented lotus blossom, Lord Vishnu asked the sage to visit a certain village on the Earth where a simple farmer, lived by the bank of the river Ganges. The sage was shocked out of his pride. How could a poor farmer rank first among the devotees of Vishnu?

Feeling intense curiosity, the sage respectfully withdrew from Lord Vishnu and journeyed to Earth. As he approached the house of the farmer he was received with great hospitality and respect. The farmer served the sage with sincere love and reverence, and requested him to stay for several days. The sage was pleased and remained there for some time, watching the activities of the Farmer.

The farmer's habit was to rise early every morning, say aloud God's name once, and then go to attend his work in the fields. When returning home in the evening after completing his day's work, he would carefully serve the sage his evening meal and before retiring to bed once again utter God's holy name. The sage carefully observed the farmer's routine for two or three days and was very disappointed.

He wondered how Lord Vishnu could take this farmer, who chanted the name of God only twice a day, to be such a great devotee. After another day he left the farmer and went straight to Lord Vishnu, and recounted all that he had seen in the company of the farmer. In amazement the sage asked the Lord how He could consider that farmer to be a special devotee.

Lord Vishnu then handed the sage a cup of oil filled to the brim and requested him to circumambulate the spiritual city and return to Him without spilling a drop of oil. As directed by the Lord, the sage took the cup in his hands and walked slowly and carefully with great concentration, and after some time returned to the presence of the Lord without spilling even one drop of oil. Upon seeing him return, the Lord asked, "How many times did you remember Me during the period of your circumambulation with the cup of oil?" The sage was a little embarrassed and surprised at this question and said, "My Lord, are You joking with me? How is it possible to remember anything else when carrying out such a difficult task? My entire mind was centered on the cup so that I might not spill a drop."

Lord Vishnu laughed at the sage's reply and remarked, "Consider the case of the farmer. He is engaged in hundreds of activities, carrying the heavy responsibilities of his worldly life. Yet in spite of all this, he does not fail to remember Me at least twice a day; whereas in the short period when you were engaged in carrying the cup of oil, you utterly forgot Me." This reply from Lord Vishnu humbled the sage.

He realized that the Lord was right, and that he had been mistaken in thinking that he was superior to all other devotees. Quality is more important than quantity, and humility is the most prominent indication of substantial spiritual attainment. For as much as we are truly in connection with the infinite, proportionately we shall feel humbled by the great mystery that is our Lord. In this connection Lord Chaitanya has given us this valuable instruction:

> trnad api sunicena
> taror api sahishnuna
> amanina manadena
> kirtaniyah sada hari

"One who considers himself to be lower than the grass, who is more tolerant than a tree, and who does not expect personal honor but is always prepared to give all respect to others, can continually chant the holy name of the Lord."

Siksastikam 3

THE THIEF AND THE SAGE

There once was a thief named Valmiki who robbed all who passed through a lonely section of a particular forest. One day the sage Narada was walking along that forest path singing the holy names of God as he played upon his stringed musical instrument called the vina. The thief could hear him calling from a distance, *"Raghupati raghava raja Ram"* as he strummed his vina.

From behind a tree the robber fell upon the sage, and attempted to run away with the vina. The sage quickly convinced the thief how sinful it was to commit robberies, after which the thief replied, "I am doing this only to feed my family. My children are hungry and my wife needs to buy cloth." The sage said to him, "Go and ask your wife and children if they will share in the karmic reactions for the sins you are committing." The words of the sage touched the heart of the thief, and thinking on the matter for a moment, he agreed to the sage's proposal. Straight away he went to his house and said to his wife and children, "A saint passing by has asked me to inquire if you are prepared to share the sins of all the robberies which I commit to feed all of you." They replied, "We cannot share your sins; how you get money is not our concern."

When the thief returned to the sage, he fell prostrate before him and said, "Please help me to give up my sinful way of life!" The sage was pleased, and requested him to always repeat the holy name of Rama. He said, "If you chant this holy name you will be freed of all sinful reactions, and in time you will attain spiritual perfection." At first the thief could not properly repeat the name and began to chant it in the opposite way as "Mara, Mara," but in time this came to resemble the holy name

"Rama,Rama" and had a purifying effect on his heart. From that day on he gave up his sinful life and went to the bank of a river to repeat the holy names in solitude. After many years the former thief became a great saint and established an ashram with many disciples. He then became known as the sage Valmiki.

Some time later as Valmiki walked along the riverbank, he came to a grove of trees where he saw two beautiful birds sporting and singing joyfully. Suddenly the male bird fell down dead, pierced by a hunter's arrow. The female bird cried out in lamentation to see her lover dead on the ground. Seeing this, the saint shouted out a curse. "You cruel hunter—as you have killed these beautiful and gentle birds, I curse you to wander homeless for the rest of your days!" Quickly the saint recovered his composure and was wonderstruck that he had lost himself to anger. He thought to himself, "What right have I to curse another? Why was I so overcome by emotion?"

As the saint reflected upon the words of his curse, he marveled at the rhythm of the words and realized that his pity had taken shape in a beautiful poetic verse. Later as the saint deeply meditated within himself, Brahma, the creator of the universe, appeared to him within his rapture. Brahma said, "Fear not, O saint; these things have taken place in order to inspire you to record the holy pastimes of Lord Rama, the Personality of Godhead. This poetic verse (shloka). has arisen from your sorrow (shoka). In this rhythm and meter the story should be told. I shall empower you with the mystic vision to see all that has occurred. You shall envision the characters as they looked, and even know their thoughts. With my blessings you shall sing this history for the benefit of the world. As long as the mountains stand and the rivers flow, so shall the epic Ramayana be cherished among men and save them from sin."

The saint Valmiki then repeated the verse over and over again to fix its pattern fully within his mind, and composing the

Ramayana in that meter, later taught it to his disciples. This is how the holy Valmiki-Ramayana was recorded for the spiritual benefit of humanity, as the following verse demonstrates.

dharmera vandhane abadha jyotirmaya rishira
e jagate satsanga karena anveshana
ta dera nishkalanka karunahrdaya jene
sakalei karaena pujana

"The effulgent sages in this world are wedded to dharma, and seek association only with the good; they are kind-hearted and spotless and are therefore worshipped by all."

Valmiki-Ramayana

MERCIFUL ARE THE WISE

The sage Narada was once traveling upon the face of the Earth singing the glories of God. Sometimes he would pass through many villages and enlighten the people about bhakti-yoga, the highest type of yoga, which is expressed as the soul's natural love for God. The villagers would always know when the sage was approaching because they would hear him strumming his vina and singing the names of God, "*Radhika-Ramana, Radhika-Ramana.*"

One day the sage approached a village and all the people came out to greet him—all but one. She was a mother who had lost her only child. In the madness of her burning grief, she wandered from house to house asking everyone to do something to bring her dead son back to life. The villagers told her there was no chance of her son returning from the dead, but her grief would not let her rest. The sage, seeing the poor woman and feeling great compassion, called her to his side. The woman recognized the sage and offered him respect, and then in all earnestness begged him to restore her son's life.

The sage agreed to restore the life of the boy if the woman could bring to him a handful of rice from a house in which no death had occurred. Wasting no time she quickly ran from house to house begging a handful of rice, but just as she was about to receive the rice, she told them the condition that no one should have died in that house. Disappointed, each villager said that death had indeed visited their house, and in fact the quantity of those who had died was greater than those who were still living.

After some time the woman realized the condition was impossible to fulfill, as death had touched the lives of everyone in the village. Feeling compassion for the loss of the other villagers, she gave up her own grief and, returning to the sage she thanked him. The sage then said to the woman:

> dehino 'smin yatha dehe
> kaumaram yauvanam jara
> tatha dehantara-praptir
> dharas tatra na muhyati

"As the embodied living soul gradually passes in this body from childhood to youth to old age, similarly that soul attains yet another body at death. The learned are not bewildered by such a transformation."

Bhagavad-gita 2.13

PRIDE AND ABILITY

Narada once thought within himself that he had mastered the whole art and science of music. Lord Vishnu, the indwelling spiritual witness of all souls, could understand the sage's mind, and therefore to curb his pride, the Lord invited him to visit the abode of the demigods. They entered a beautiful palace where they found numerous men and women weeping over the condition of their arms and legs.

Lord Vishnu stopped and asked them the reason for their lamentation. They answered that they were the personified musical ragas and raginis created by Shiva, but that a sage by the name of Narada—ignorant of the true knowledge of music and unskilled in performance—had sung them recklessly, and thus their features were distorted and their limbs broken; and that unless Shiva or some other skillful person sings them properly, there was no hope of their ever being restored to their former state of body.

The sage, feeling ashamed, knelt before Lord Vishnu and realized he had overestimated his abilities. By the grace of the Lord, at that moment he recalled this instruction:

raso 'ham apsu kaunteya
prabhasmi shashi-suryayoh
pranavah sarva-vedeshu
shabdah khe paurusham nrshu

"O son of Kunti, I am the taste of water, the light of the sun and the moon, and the syllable Om in the Vedic mantras. I am the sound in ether and the ability in man."

Bhagavad-gita 7.8

LORD KRISHNA

Near the city of Mathura, some men were holding a seven-day public reading of the scriptures which describe the eternal pastimes of Lord Krishna. The man reciting the scriptures was describing that Krishna is very highly decorated with all kinds of jewels when He goes to tend the cows in the forest.

By chance a thief was attending that reading, and heard of the jewels adorning Krishna's spiritual body, he thought to himself, "Why not go to the town of Braja and plunder this boy? He's in the forest wearing so many valuable jewels. I can go there and catch this child and take all his jewels." He began seriously thinking that in one night he would become a wealthy man. This feeling intensified, and with great eagerness and anxiety he began to think, "I must see Krishna! I must see Krishna!"

With this deep desire he went to Braja, and sitting by the bank of the Yamuna river, he chanted, "Krishna, Krishna." For many days and nights the thief remained awake chanting whithout eating or drinking anything. Finally one night, Krishna appeared before him just as the man reciting the scriptures had described. The thief then said," O Krishna, You are such a nice boy," thinking that if he flattered Krishna it would be easy to steal all of His jewelry. Then he said frankly, "You are so rich; may I take some of Your ornaments? "No, no," said Krishna. "My mother will be very angry with Me! I cannot give them away." Of course Krishna knew his intention, but He was playing just like a helpless child. Hearing this the thief's anxiety increased, but by Krishna's association he was becoming mysteriously purified of material desires.

Then at last Krishna said, "Alright you can take My jewels." But by now the thief had become so purified by Krishna's merciful glance that he no longer desired the jewels. He said, "My dear Krishna, I no longer desire any worldly wealth, but only the wealth of service to You. Please accept me as Your devotee." Within himself he realized his great fortune to come in connection with the Lord, and recalled one verse spoken by the sage Durvasa which he had heard from the man reciting scripture:

yan-nama-shruti-matrena
puman bhavati nirmalah
tasya tîrtha-padha kim va
dasanam avashishyate

"A man becomes purified simply by hearing the holy name
of the Supreme Personality of Godhead, whose lotus feet
create all the holy places of pilgrimage. Therefore what
remains to be attained by those who
have become His servants?"

Srimad-Bhagavatam 9.5.1

GOOD ASSOCIATION

Thousands of years ago in a time long forgotten, there once was a discussion between two sages, one older and one younger. The old sage stated that the power of austerities was greater than the company of saints. The young sage disagreed with him, and suggested that they take the matter to Lord Vishnu. Lord Vishnu directed them to Ananta, the multi-headed spiritual serpent upon whom the material universes rest.

The sages approached Ananta and asked Him which was greater— the company of saints or the performance of austerities. Ananta said, "I have the weight of the entire Earth on My head. If you will lift it from My head for a moment, I will be free to answer your question." The two sages looked at each other and considered how this problem might be solved. The old sage suggested that he could apply the power he had gained by his austerities and lift the Earth.

He then applied all his strength, but the Earth did not move. Seeing this, the young sage came forward, and putting forth all the strength that he had acquired by one moment's association with saints, lifted the Earth. Ananta then spoke the following verse to the sages:

sadhu-sanga sadhu sanga sarva shastre kaya
lava matra sadhu sange sarva siddhi haya

"The verdict of all revealed scriptures is that even by
a moment's association with a saint,
one can attain all perfection."

Chaitanya-Charitamrita, M.22.54

SHIVA'S MEDITATION

High on Mount Kailas there was once a talk between Shiva and his beautiful consort Parvati. Mother Parvati asked her great husband, "What is the greatest form of worship?" Shiva then replied,

aradhananam sarvesham
vishnor aradhanam param

"My dear Devi, although the Vedas recommend the worship
of demigods, the worship of Lord Vishnu is the topmost."
Hearing this, Parvati became a little disappointed, thinking,
"I am constantly serving Lord Shiva, and thus I am not doing
the highest worship." Lord Shiva then gave the second
half of the verse:

tasmat prarataram devi
tadiyanam samachanam

"However, above the worship of Lord Vishnu is
the rendering of service to devotees who are related to Vishnu."

Laghu-bhagavatamrta 2.4

Hearing this Parvati smiled, thinking, "My Lord Shiva is the greatest devotee of Lord Vishnu, whose divine feet he always meditates upon. Therefore I am truly performing the highest form of worship." Then the beautiful Parvati recalled this verse from the Vedic scriptures:

nimnaganam yatha ganga
devanam achyuto yatha
vaishnavanam yatha shambhu
purananam idam tatha

"Of all rivers, the Ganges is the best. Of all the
powerful lords of the universe, Lord Vishnu is
the best. Of all Puranas, this Bhagavat-purana is
the best, and of all the devotees of the Supreme Lord,
Shiva is the best."

Srimad-Bhagavatam 12.13.16

DEATH APPROACHING

lexander the Great accumulated vast amounts of wealth by
waging wars. He conquered and looted other countries, and in
the process killed thousands of people. Although in his time he
was considered the richest man on Earth and a great king, he was
also greedy, selfish, and cruel. But when his death approached,
he told his men, "I have killed so many people and sinned
greatly in order to gather all of my wealth. But now my death is
approaching and I must leave my body and all this wealth related
to it. I will leave this life without a single coin. When my body
is taken to the grave, see that my two hands are stretched out,
palms open and exposed to view, while the rest of my body is
covered, so that the people might see that I, a great king and the
richest man in the world, have gone on, leaving this life without
a single coin. All possessions that are in connection with the
temporary material body have no lasting value, and all sensual
pleasures eventually bring suffering as a reaction. Therefore it
is wise to refrain from overindulgence in worldly pursuits." The
scriptures similarly guide us in this way:

ye hi samsparsha ja boga
duhka-yonaya eva te
ady-antavantah kaunteya
na teshu ramate budhah

"An intelligent person does not take part in the sources of
misery, which are due to contact with the objects of the senses.
O son of Kunti, the so-called pleasures produced by such actions
have a beginning and end, and so the wise
do not delight in them."

Bhagavad-gita 5.22

AJAMILA

In the city of Kanya-kubja there lived a saintly young brahmin
named Ajamila. Once, Ajamila was sent to the forest by his father
to collect leaves and twigs and wood for a fire. While in the forest
he came upon a prostitute, and by contemplating her attractive
features, lusty desires were soon awakened within his heart. This
progression of contemplation and attraction is described in the
scriptures:

dhyato visayan pumsa
sangas tesupajayate
sangat sanjayate kama
kamat krodho bhijayate

"While contemplating the objects of the senses,
one develops attachment for them. From such
attachment lust develops, and from lust,
anger arises."

Bhagavad-gita 2.62

By repeated association with that prostitute, Ajamila gradually lost all of his saintly qualities, and leaving his brahminical family, he began to earn his livelihood by gambling and stealing. He took up residence with the prostitute and fathered ten children by her. Just to maintain them all, Ajamila became increasingly involved in criminal activities and thus passed eighty-eight years of his life in this way.

Of the ten sons of Ajamila, the baby named Narayana was the favorite due to being the youngest. Because the child would crawl about the floor and speak in broken language, Ajamila's mind was constantly absorbed in affectionate thoughts of the child. If he could not see Narayana he would immediately begin calling for him. When Ajamila would take his meals, he would call his son Narayana to come and eat with him, and the young child would carefully imitate the movements of his father. Thus Ajamila would spend most of his time with the boy and constantly call his name.

Because the name of Narayana is one of the holy names of Lord Vishnu and is therefore spiritually potent, Ajamila became purified by repeatedly chanting it. Even though his intention was to call his son Narayana, still, he received pious credit for chanting the name of God. This is known as *ajnata-sukriti,* or accumulation of unknown pious credit.

Due to Ajamila's advanced age, the time of death eventually arrived. As Ajamila lay upon his bed in a semi-conscious state, he perceived three grotesque subtle beings approaching him. Their facial features were fierce and twisted, and in their hands they carried ropes with which to bind Ajamila and bring him to the abode of their master. These fearsome spirits were the servants of Yama-raj, the lord of death who punishes all sinful persons in the material world. Sinful activities are performed with the body, mind, and speech, and therefore there were three of these servants known as Yama-dutas.

When Ajamila saw them approach he became extremely frightened, and with tears in his eyes he began to call out "Narayana! Narayana!" He did not intend to call the holy name of God, but was actually referring to his son Narayana. However, because at the point of death Ajamila had inoffensively called the holy name of God in complete helplessness, the servants of Lord Vishnu known as the Vishnu-dutas immediately appeared there after hearing the name of their master.

They did not consider that Ajamila was actually calling for his son because he had chanted the name of the Lord in a helpless condition, and by the strength of that chanting, he was eligible for liberation from the reactions of his past sinful deeds. This is not actually pure chanting of the holy name, but because the Lord is infinite and absolute, His holy name is therefore nondifferent from His absolute spiritual personality, and even indirectly chanting that name can bring all good fortune to the living entities of this world. In voices that resounded like thunder, the Vishnu-dutas forbade the servants of Yama-raj from snatching the soul of Ajamila.

The Yama-dutas felt frustration because of being checked from their duty, and could recognize the superiority of the Vishnu-dutas, whose astonishing beauty shone forth with a gorgeous transcendental splendor. Their eyes resembled lotus petals and they were adorned with opulent jewelry, helmets, and weapons. They appeared spiritually youthful and their brilliance illuminated all directions. With some trepidation the Yama-dutas then asked, "Who are you great personalities? We can see by your appearance that you are either demigods or great devotees of the Lord, and as such, surely you must know that we are deputed by our master Yama-raj to arrest all sinful souls. Being aware of these facts, why have you forbade us to touch this man Ajamila?"

The wonderful servants of Lord Vishnu then smiled broadly and replied, "If you are truly the servants of Yama-raj, then explain to us the true meaning of religion as well as the symptoms of irreligion. What is the process of punishing sinners and who are the actual candidates for such punishment? Are all persons engaged in fruitive activities punishable, or only a select few?"

The Yama-dutas then replied: devotional activities which are recommended in the vedic scriptures are revelations from the unconditioned absolute spiritual reality. These activities are meant to reawaken the dormant love of Godhead which is the natural function of all living souls. Just as the nature of fire is to emit heat and light, or the nature of water is liquidity, similarly it is the inherent nature of the eternal spirit soul to love.

That natural loving propensity of the soul can only reach its fully blossomed state when directed towards the Absolute reality Lord Vishnu, Narayana, or Krishna, for only God can infinitely reciprocate the love of the soul. Unfortunately, human beings conditioned by the material energies forget this basic truth of existence, and so fall into the whirlpool of viscious fruitive activities which bear as their bitter fruit such painfull circumstances as birth, disease, old age and death.

The fruitive activities indulged in by living souls who are devoid of spiritual truth, are considered impious and selfish and are therefore punishable by the universal laws of karma. This situation is inescapable for the soul, for all activities are witnessed by the sun and moon, evening, day and night, fire, sky, water, land, air, and ultimately by God who is situated as the all-pervading Supersoul witness, in the hearts of all living beings. In proportion to the extent of one's pious or impious actions in this life, one must enjoy or suffer the corresponding reactions in the next life. Just as springtime in the present indicates the nature of springtimes in the past and future, so this life of happiness, distress or a mixture of both gives evidence concerning the pious or impious activities of one's past and future lives. As a sleeping person acts according to the body manifested in his dreams and accepts it to be himself, so one identifies with his present body, which he aquired because of his past pious or impious actions, and is therefore conditioned and unable to know of his past or future lives.

The Vishnu-duttas who were beautifully effulgent by emanating rays of spiritual light then smilingly admonished the servants of Yama-raj in a tone that was both commanding yet compassionate. The servants of Lord Vishnu said: Dear servants of Yama-raj, what you have stated regarding the conditioned piety and impiety of living beings, and their resulting karmic punishment is certainly true. Yet, there is a higher authority than the universal justice of karmic laws. That higher authority is the mercy of the Absolute Godhead Who is ever inviting the fallen materially conditioned souls to rejoin Him in His eternal spiritual pastimes of loving exchange.

Certainly Ajamila has performed many sinful and impious deeds in the course of his present life, and for this he would normally be punished by your master Yama-raj, and the stringent laws of material nature. Yet this man Ajamila has, in a helpless state called out the spiritually potent name of the Absolute Reality, Narayana. Ajamila called out that holy name offenslessly, without any personal motivation for gain, and although he did not chant purely, he has nevertheless attracted the attention of our Lord. He is therefore purified of not only the reactions of his present sinful life, but also those of many millions of lives. He is now eligible for promotion to the spiritual atmosphere.

By following ritualistic religious ceremonies or undergoing severe austerities and penance, sinful people do not become as purified as by chanting only once the holy names of Lord Vishnu such as Narayana. Although ritualistic atonement may free one from sinful reactions, it does not actually awaken the soul's love of God, unlike the chanting of the Lord's holy names, which awakens affectionate remmemberance of the Lord's fame, qualities, attributes, beautiful pastimes and paraphernalia. This man is now blameless, do not try to take him to your master for punishment.

After the servants of Yama-raj had been forbidden by the Vishnu-duttas to take away the soul of Ajamila, they quickly went to their master and related to him all that had taken place. Having been released from the fearful custody of the Yama-dutas, Ajamila felt great relief for he had witnessed how the beautiful servants of lord Vishnu had saved him. Trembling with great awe and humility, the delighted Ajamila respectfully bowed to the shinning Vishnu-duttas who noticed he was attempting to say something, and then suddenly disappeared from his presence. This was done to increase the feelings of gratitude that Ajamila now felt towards the Lord.

Ajamila said: Oh! How foolish and degraded I became! By overindulging my senses I commited many sinful acts. Simply to satisfy my tongue I have cruelly killed so many creatures. How wretched it is that one living being should maintain his life by unnecessarily slaughtering hundreds of other lives. Alas, by my sinful actions I have degraded my family tradition. I left my beautiful and chaste wife and begot children in the womb of a degraded prostitute who was unclean and accustomed to drinking wine.

My father and mother were old and had no other son or freind to look after them, they lived alone with great difficulty, yet I ungratefully left them in that condition. It is clear to me that as a consequence of such cruel activities, one must fall down into hellish conditions and suffer extreme miseries. Was this a dream? Where have those radiant angelic beings gone who saved me from the hands of the devilish servants of Yama-raj, the lord of death? It is by the greatest fortune and the mercy of God, that I have witnessed these things and obtained another chance in life.

Since I have recieved this great opportunity to change my life, I must now completely control my mind and senses, and always engage in devotional service to the Lord so that I may be saved from again falling into a degraded way of life. By identifying oneself with the gross material body, one is subjected to unlimited desires, the pursuit of which necessitates many types of pious and impious activities. This is the cause of material bondage. Now I shall attempt to disentangle myself from these illusory pursuits by renouncing all lusty desires, becomming a freindly well-wisher to all living entities and constantly remmembering the Holy Names of God such as Narayana, Rama, Vishnu and Krishna.

Thereafter, with great determination Ajamila detached himself from the material conception of life which had caused him so much trouble. He traveled to the city of Hardwar near the Himalayan mountains and took shelter of a Vishnu temple there. By adopting the process of bhakti-yoga he fully controlled his senses and applied his mind and body to the service of the Lord. Many years later death once again approached the now saintly Ajamila. At the moment of death as his consciousness departed his material body, he once again saw those spiritually radiant and angelic servants of Lord Vishnu, and himself attained a beautiful spiritual form just appropriate for an associate of the Lord. Accompanied by the servants of Lord Vishnu, Ajamila assended to the spiritual sky and the abode of Lord Vishnu, the husband of the goddess of fortune.

Ajamila was a brahmin who had lost all of his spiritual merit by the pernicious effects of bad association. Yet even greater spiritual merit was regained by the power and mercy of the Lord's Holy Names. Therefore, one who desires positive spiritual attainment and freedom from material bondage must certainly adopt the habit of chanting and glorifying the holy names, forms and pastimes of the Lord, as well as serving the Lord's saintly devotee'sOne cannot derive true benefit from other methods, such as pious activities and atonement, the accumulation of knowledge or meditation in mystic yoga, because even after following such methods one will inevitably adopt fruitive activities again, unable to control the mind which is colored by the base qualities of nature such as passion and ignorance. Thus, many great authorities direct us to seek the Lord's mercy by constantly chanting His holy names.

harer nama harer nama harer nama eva kevalam
kalau nasty eva nasty eva nasty eva gatir anyatha

The name of the Lord, the name of the Lord,
the name of the Lord is absolutely the
only way, the only way, the only way in this
degraded age. There is absolutely no other way.

*Caitanya-Caritamṛta adi 17.21,
from Brihanaradeya Upanishada*

Upon the Wheel

An Original Poem by Matthew F. Bennett

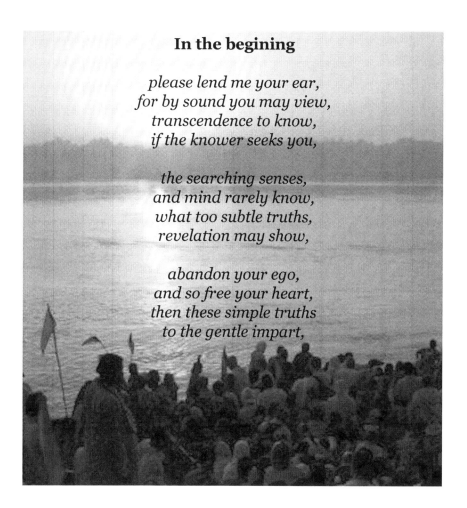

In the begining

please lend me your ear,
for by sound you may view,
transcendence to know,
if the knower seeks you,

the searching senses,
and mind rarely know,
what too subtle truths,
revelation may show,

abandon your ego,
and so free your heart,
then these simple truths
to the gentle impart,

113

and now to disclose,
what lay at the root;
the unconditioned,
supreme absolute,

so true to be sure,
the godhead is one,
yet absolute engendered,
forms does not shun,

in all-loving pastimes,
so playful and pure,
the paragon of truth,
is not He but a Her,

in conscious abodes,
of beauty and light,
the angels do serve,
for this couples' delight,

from Their halo of truth,
sweet beauty divine,
dance unlimited angels,
with a countenance fine,

and thus they emerge,
beyond birth and death,
who subsist upon love,
not dependent on breath,

not twain of the heart,
one pointed in sight,
eternal, aware,
and filled with delight,

this angel of spirit,
no base earthly form,
from one now the many,
she comes and is born,

born yet unborn,
she did not begin,
o'er the soul thats emerging,
death never does win,

no weapons divide her,
no water does wet,
nor fire can burn,
what the earth not beget,

and then come to pass,
though most do remain,
still others do slip,
from loves' sweet refrain,

then slipping thus,
from the sweet absolute,
enchained by the senses,
the spirit is mute,

feeling earth, water, fire,
and all that is air,
to mix in a form,
that's heavy with care,

these caught in a basket,
bound up in skin,
when you solve this riddle,
you'll never begin,

these angels do pass,
through unlimited rounds,
of birth, age, and death,
with a wailing resound,

Upon the wheel

I am such a one,
please hear my tale
I've borne the horn,
the claw and the scale,

the birth that came first,
as a god ever fair,
in mirth and in play,
I had not a care,

yet actions propel,
and soon was I drawn,
to forms I would rue,
and the pain that they spawn,

action breeds action,
pleasure calls pain,
by gaining you lose,
and losing you gain,

the bright rolling thunder,
then slipped from my hand,
I next lost my wings,
and fell to the land,

116

in a raindrop rush,
I fell from the sky,
to a greener blush,
'pon the grass I lie,

these powers lost I,
to a seed next encased,
imobile and mute,
my wisdom erased,

then did alight,
all feathered and fair,
consumed I thus,
to the egg did repair,

with a peep breaking forth,
by the beak and the wing,
upon the tall treetops,
so feathered I sing,

then swooping low,
I fell to the claw,
my back was torn open
by mean beastly jaw,

my next role to play,
'pon this earthly stage,
was a feline eye,
and cunning rage,

upon many small creatures,
then did I feast,
ashamed that now I,
had become such a beast,

being eaten then passing,
from semen to womb,
each birth is a doorway,
that leads to a tomb,

Mercy

once while I roamed,
in search of my prey,
as the sun it did set,
'pon the fast waning day,

then did I see,
small flickering light,
bright votive lamp,
that rent the black night,

in smooth wary steps,
with a feline paw,
approaching the lamp,
'twas butter I saw,

butter, yes burning,
in place of the oil,
my dry thirsty tongue,
the content did soil,

at this the small lamp,
did flicker so bright,
I had to run off,
in quick hasty fright,

that small votive flame,
offered up to the God,
I did so enhance,
by my thirsty prod,

and this brought good fruit,
'tis true, and a fact,
unaware that I gained,
this small pious act,

I had no intent,
to give service to God,
but He in His mercy,
gave a wink and a nod,

forever He searches,
in pity to give,
the highest reward,
to all that do live,

sweet God ever smiling,
benedicted me so;
"Only one more base birth,
as a beast shall he go",

and so did begin,
my new found ascent,
for in the strong jaws,
of a bear was I rent,

that bear was soon slain,
by hunter so rude,
who consumed all the flesh,
thus I entered his brood,

Awakened

next passing through,
this hunter did go,
to tight mothers womb,
and a feeling of woe,

whilst I locked within,
that chamber so tight,
I now was aware,
of my perilous plight,

and praying so true,
to the good God of love,
"please let me ascend,
once more to above,

I promise to seek thee,
in next my new frame,
by chanting your glories,
and singing your name"

myself thus resigned,
when next did emerge,
as still but a youth,
my heart did I purge,

hot anger and greed,
and lust that is base,
I laboured in vain,
to my sin all erase,

for by the true wisdom,
that descends from on high,
my last beastly births,
I still yet could spy,

and so I to save,
and now change my fate,
I quick stole away,
as the hours grew late,

my parents they ever,
did search me in vain,
it was not my goal,
to so cause them pain,

the hearts's high ideal,
quite often does spawn,
a wee fledgling chick,
to the tall graceful swan,

for a child may ask a mother
the mother ask a son
the son may ask the father
but the father may have none

the student asks the teacher
the people ask the king
the robber asks his victim
but no answer they could bring

the doctor asks his patient
the patient asks a priest
priests ask the scripture
which makes them ask again

a patron asks a merchant
the merchant asks his goods
they make no sound at all
so then he asks the woods

while in the woods
he settled down
his mind it was quite still
for then the spirit dawned in him
and soon he found the will

to give himself unto his Lord
in many selfless deeds
and found a joy within himself
that love of God does breed

and so this boy,
did set out alone,
with stout burning breast,
and a face that e're shone,

to soon find a teacher,
that be wise and so true,
and now set his step,
upon the long path anew,

through forests so dark,
and high rugged hill,
this youth forged ahead,
armed only with will,

Retrograde

till I came to a river,
and fell down to rest,
and spied a fair maid,
with milky white breast,

while washing her cloth,
she glanced at my youth,
her beauty so fair,
I felt quite uncouth,

but spoke I did thus,
for my heart could not wait,
and the passion that burns,
I did then relate,

forgetting my oath,
my senses ran wild,
for reason was shadowed,
by this beautiful child,

and taking her hand,
she lay near a stone,
beneath shady trees,
her pleasure was known,

from the seed of desire,
comes the fruit that is grief,
it would be a long time,
till I came to relief,

then led to the village,
her relations I met,
their company dull,
I soon would regret,

for round a great oak,
all came for a feast,
with abandon and folly,
they roasted a beast,

my tongue I denied,
for killing is wrong,
and took only grains,
but joined in their song,

as night beconed slumber,
'pon these companions of late,
I quick stole away,
for her kiss did not wait,

for I knew if I tarried,
my goal I would lose,
and love over lust,
was what I must choose,

not love of this world,
nor possesions to gain,
will comfort the heart,
like the senses in rein,

for then will the light,
that's hidden within,
come to the fore,
and joy will begin,

those deities and,
their planet forms,
those stars that often,
herald storms,

we bow to you,
and ask your grace,
from high above,
or inner space,

ordained you are,
with thankless task,
return to me,
the woes of past,

great demigods
and men reside,
within this world,
together tied,

in union we,
bring forth our fate,
no one to blame,
to curse nor hate,

On my way

I regretted her loss,
but again on my way,
resolve did grow stronger,
with each passing day,

till sages I found,
in the forest remote,
who lived on but milk,
and the butter of goat,

they taught me their secrets,
and practice arcane,
till I so excelled,
their affection did wane,

for jealousy sprouted,
in the heart of their chief,
I much did regret,
as the source of their grief,

their teaching was this:
that the soul there is none,
when things come apart,
all return to the one,

this did not bring,
much joy to my heart,
and thinking I thus,
did their company part,

grateful I was,
for the care and succor,
yet I knew in my heart,
there's sure to be more,

The dream

again I did wander,
by night and by day,
how far I had travelled,
I still cannot say,

till in my fatigue,
below trees I did lay,
so slumbering thus,
throughout all the day,

another life,
I live unseen,
passing me by,
these sleepy dreams,

the minds' absorption,
of days' cognition,
by sleep constructs,
a new rendition,

wild wonderous dreams,
my mind then did show,
as I lay asleep,
subtle actions did sow,

and thus seeing through,
these dreams of the day,
myself I did view,
in a very strange way,

with beard all of grey,
and velvety gown,
upon mighty steed,
did prance all around,

the steed it did buck,
and throw to the ground,
with pain to my head,
I came swiftly down,

with mind still awake,
quick seeing and free,
i then saw my body,
beneath that green tree,

and I wondered thus:
how is it so?
that I should now sleep,
though asleep I did know,

that my body does lay,
so still on the ground,
yet I moving free,
like the air so unbound!

am I yet dead?
is this body now slain?
how can it be thus,
I am now in twain?

while thinking I this,
I then spied a light,
and as it drew closer,
'twas ever more bright,

and soon drawing near,
I saw past the glow,
and could just percieve,
a form it did show,

so clearly now,
it came into view,
a tall regal form,
with bright golden hue,

who's eyes did shine,
with celestial glow,
a countanance fair,
of compassion did show,

one hand it did raise,
this angelic form,
and then it did speak,
this rare one unborn,

"greetings! young friend,
tis good fortune so true,
that now should I speak,
these words unto you,

I know that your heart,
its contents burn bright,
you seek now to wed,
your soul to the light,

with good high intent,
abandoning home,
in woodland and meadow,
and mountains you roam,

and shun what most others,
hold ever so dear,
and free from desire,
your path is now clear,

so please listen now,
my words you will hear,
to comfort your heart,
and alay all your fear,

what you now seek,
you ever yet are,
strange but so true,
we ourselves do but mar,

the minds' understanding,
of eternal self,
is clouded with care,
for the body's own health,

this matter of earth,
is not what we are,
but we thinking thus,
our vision does mar,

and then to fall through,
birth and death as it seems,
yet in the bold truth,
they are but our dreams,

so please seek it not,
pale fortune in hand,
lest you become chained,
to this dark mortal land,

see here my young friend,
seek destiny high,
shun all that is base,
going behind the "I",

and unlock your heart,
past material view,
there waits a true love,
that's inviting you,

not of the body,
or forms it is based,
but bright selfless love,
can the ego erase,

and thus I come now,
to give you a start,
on the eternal journey,
to that spiritual heart,

dig not your treasure,
by actions so base,
nor by much endeavor,
great knowledge to chase,

nor austerities vain,
that 'ere leads to naught,
and by such great pain,
and troubles are fraught,

but yes! do go seek,
saints wise and so rare,
serving God first,
do live without care,

attending such souls,
without thought of a gain,
you'll soon find a joy,
when love comes to reign,

and now please do hear,
holy sound that is pure,
for all worldly pains,
is surely the cure,

always repeat these,
with every life breath,
this sweet holy sound,
can free you from death,

for death the illusion,
no power does show,
o'er the simple and wise,
that divinity know,

make your soul clear,
as the bright morning sun,
drawn by affection,
to the abode of the One,

above the creator,
beyond the destroyer,
serve the maintainer,
the soul of all souls,

turn your tears inside,
to the flower within,
tis norished by goodness,
and trampled by sin,

by affection and mercy,
by good service you win,
the ever bright station,
where you never begin,

the master of mystics,
the trickster, the thief,
playing His flute,
steals the heart of all souls,

an autocrat and magician,
the weaver of dreams,
the watcher, the taker,
the talkative child,

He laughs as they bow,
and winks as they call,
His nature is beauty,
the attractor of all",

and so speaking thus,
that spirit did smile,
and beams of bright light,
shone upon me awhile,

near such a one,
was I humbled and meek,
then trembling thus,
I laboured to speak,

seeing my intent,
the vision withdrew,
and I left alone,
no trace of that view,

just then a red apple,
fell down on my head,
and startled did rise,
from my grassy bed,

and pondering long,
a strange mystic muse,
it was not deception,
nor mere earthly ruse,

with deep gratitute,
just then newly found,
I began to practice,
the revealed holy sound,

that was now conveyed,
in wonderous dream,
by bright gracious spirit,
just now unseen.

ABOUT THE AUTHOR

In the spring of 1985, as a young man in search of answers, Matthew Bennett traveled alone to India and met his Gurudeva, the venerable sanskrit scholar, vaisnava saint, and eminent Vedic Acharya- Srila Sridhar Maharaja (1895-1988). The following year, on the banks of the holy Ganges river, Matthew was initiated into the brahminical lineage of priest-teachers, and given the name Matura Nath das. Inspired by the deep wisdom and devotion of his Gurudeva, Matura has engaged in educational outreach programs for the past 28 years. He has taught over 1200 classes and led numerous kirtans in India, England, Australia and America.

As an Ayurvedic Counselor certified by The American Institute of Vedic Studies under Dr. David Frawley, Matura assists others to find clarity and growth through the insight born of self-awareness, Ayurveda and Vedic Devotional Yoga. Matura has dedicated his life to helping others heal body, mind and spirit in order to assist in the achievement of greater levels of satisfaction and success in all areas of life.

For more information or to schedule a private consultation.

Please visit
www.abundantlives.org

Matura Matthew Bennett is also a multi-instrumentalist who plays sitar, harmonium, flute, and guitar. He sings a wide variety of original songs and sanskrit chants that heal, inspire and delight the soul. Songs from his new cd "Dharma Wheels" as well as his first cd "Artistic-2-Mystic can be found online at amazon, itunes, cd baby and other outlets.

His music website is: www.reverbnation.com/matura

Made in the USA
San Bernardino, CA
11 March 2017